Angelos Michalopoulos

Basking in the wrong kind of sunshine

Translation:
Angelos Michalopoulos, Andreas Machairas

ATHENS 2015

© Angelos Michalopoulos, 2015.
This publication (work, material, book) may not be reproduced, transmitted or copied in part or in whole, by any means and in any form, nor may it be translated, adapted, adjusted, converted, or otherwise circulated or communicated to the public in any way or by any means, in accordance with the provisions of L. 2121/1993 and the Berne Convention for the Protection of Literary and Artistic Works, without the prior written approval of the author.
The reproduction of the typesetting and layout, the cover and the overall aesthetic appearance of this book by photocopying, electronic or any other methods for purposes of exploitation is strictly prohibited according to article 51 of L. 2121/1993.

www.angelosm.com
email: onelilo@angelosm.com

ISBN: 978-618-81397-8-7

CHARACTERS:

GEORGE

HIS CONSCIENCE

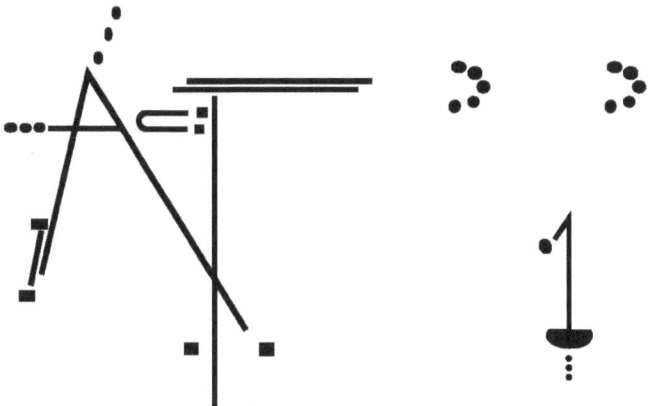

(George and his Conscience sit facing each other on two back-to-back chairs)

GEORGE: You know, I read somewhere that poets read their poems to their conscience before they begin to write them. Do you think that's true?

CONSCIENCE: What can I say? I know so much about this subject that I feel I don't know anything. What more are the words of a soul anyway than hard-working porters of their owner's conscience?

GEORGE: So, a person's sorrow is the porter of his personal darkness?

CONSCIENCE: Come on, don't play dumb with me. You know very well that every truth of yours, no matter how small or insignificant, grabs the biggest weapon she can handle and goes on patrol during most hours of the day, walking up and down in your mind, trying to protect it from yourself.

GEORGE: That's right. I have seen that weapon. Not only is it huge, the damn thing keeps on smiling all the time.

CONSCIENCE: It smiles because it knows that it doesn't need to feel any pain itself in order to kill any delusion it sees running to escape from the teeth of the reality in which you have forced your mind to live. *(Pause)*

GEORGE: Since we are talking about delusions, I don't know if you've noticed but my own are in high spirits today.

CONSCIENCE: Well, it must be one of those days…

GEORGE: I am afraid that it is one of those days when the truth will dance back and forth in the showcase I have made especially for her, so I can sell her more easily to the people I spend time with. *(He stands up)* Today I intend to have her dance until she drops to the floor unconscious.

CONSCIENCE: I am afraid that today is one of those days when your delusions are more competent not only than you but than me as well.

GEORGE: Competent in what?

CONSCIENCE: In convincing you that they are as true as your truth.

GEORGE: I hope that's not true.

CONSCIENCE: I'm in no mood to spend my day helping you figure out in which part of your previous sorrow one of those hours of your life that refuses to accept her role and become the next one is hiding out. If you pay close attention, it is the one sitting a bit further away from where the hours of your life you will use to construct your future are waiting, looking for some time now for a chance to introduce herself to you without your biggest insecurity being present.

GEORGE: You're probably right. I am afraid that she is waiting among those sad hours that know how to hide the second starting point of an even greater sorrow in their finish line.

CONSCIENCE: Maybe …

GEORGE: Every morning I see each person's enthusiasm come wake him up as gently as possible so he can get up and go meet all that will happen to him throughout the day. My own enters the room and, after first standing over me staring at me contemptuously, turns around and walks out banging the door behind it. That's why the first thing I do every morning is to throw all the dreams I didn't dream into the trash and, after I finish, throw myself in there too. It's not my sorrow's wish for me to be unable to cry, it is the bad check my anger leaves on the bedside table every evening for me to find as soon as I wake up, so during the day I can try to find at least one smile produced by the beauty of a soul that has more compassion in her than cowardice to cash it.

CONSCIENCE: Any soul?

GEORGE: In the past yes, I did not discriminate. Lately though I feel a need to know her well, because I have become quite fearful and very cautious.

CONSCIENCE: Are you frightened by the people you have to deal with or your own inability to understand them?

GEORGE: Both. You know, I feel as if I have to endlessly shuttle between the various transparent realities I have created myself to protect you from having to confront my unswerving conviction since my teenage years that I am a man made from a single material.

CONSCIENCE: You mean from a single authenticity?

GEORGE: I don't know, maybe. Can a human being have two authenticities? I always hoped that if I took any part of my life and cut it in half I would find a piece of myself made from the same material as the rest, which would consist of exactly the same ingredients, the same proportions of joy, disappointment and courage. As I was growing up, though, I began to fall in love and, without meaning to, to increasingly disappoint at the same time, those character flaws of mine that are more optimistic than me, those shortcomings which, though they were born weaker that I, managed over time to believe more in themselves than I do in mine. In them live these all powerful and cunning shadows the sun always created each time when, wanting to play with me, he swung around my body illuminating what I felt right then from different angles! Having managed to confuse and bewilder me, he would suddenly stop and, raising his hand in front of my face, point out a brand new way for me to look at myself, his way. So each time I ended up discovering in me a new character strength, more capable and stronger than me, along with a totally fresh damn wound which until then had found a way to convince me that it wasn't mine.

CONSCIENCE: What happened in the end, did you eventually figure out what you're made of? I would really like to know.

GEORGE: I am afraid that walking on the road that leads to an answer I began to hear from both sidewalks on the left and right questions I had never heard before, questions I had never thought I would ever find the strength to ask myself. The more I went on, the more I realized that I am not made from a single material, but from the same stuff that every person in the world is made of. Thus I ended up believing that we are all heroes and cowards, thieves and benefactors, violent and sensitive, stingy and generous, warriors and faint-hearted wimps.

CONSCIENCE: That's right. What determines which of these will be the final product of your actions is us, your consciences. Man can become anything, no matter how many years he has lived, even something he never expected himself to become because he was sure that he did not have the necessary materials in him to build it. It is not circumstances that determine what you become, it is us, your consciences, the lighthouses in the middle of every storm which you yourselves, since you don't want to blame your self-confidence with shaping it on your behalf, let the circumstances of your life invent. We are the lighthouses that show you not only where you should go to save yourselves, but also where you should go to escape from yourselves, or rather to escape the parts of yourselves you cannot tame because you never tried to learn exactly how they work.

GEORGE: I know what you're trying to do! Today you are hell bent on throwing me on my biggest insecurity, to force me to embrace her and make me feel her until I become one with her. You really want that, don't you? Maybe because you know that the definition of an emotional fog is what a man feels when he begins to answer the questions he has not yet dared to ask himself.

CONSCIENCE: Maybe...

GEORGE: There are so many times in my life when I feel as if I am riding one of those enormous construction machines which I am expected to operate in the next few minutes without having a clue how to do it.

CONSCIENCE: To construct something or tear it down?

GEORGE: To construct by destroying. Come on, isn't that what you've been asking me to do all my life?

CONSCIENCE: A conscience overcomes any luck, any fate, any excuse. You are what you have done, you are what you have said. A person is the sum total of his actions, the sum of his words. His mind consists of all the decisions he has made in his life, his soul of all the emotions he has already felt. These are proof of who he is. Every decision of yours is proof of who you are. When two people sit facing each other, what they see looking at their conversational partner is an endless torrent of information wrapped in highlights of their life together, streaming out of their eyes. Whatever anyone has told you, whatever he has done to you, pours out of his body without him being able to do anything to stop it, and more importantly, without him being able to do anything to make it seem more beautiful that it actually is. While you two are talking, all the truth, all the lies, all the meanness, all the violence and all the tenderness go into a box which he unwittingly deposits in front of your feet seconds before he opens his mouth.

GEORGE: It seems as if you are telling me that a person's silence contains more information about him than any of his words.

CONSCIENCE: Maybe this is the way a person starts constructing the road that connects his soul with that of the person he is talking to. *(Pause)*

GEORGE: You know, I have managed to reach the end of this road only a few times in my life.

CONSCIENCE: Of course, because every day of his life a person adds new pieces to what he is, learning more about himself through each new action of his, each new word he utters.

GEORGE: I really like what you are telling me. *(Pause)* But it also really scares me.

CONSCIENCE: Hence, at the end of every phrase you utter, every action you complete, you unwittingly go and sit at a narrow, extremely uncomfortable school desk waiting for your own words, your own actions, to explain to you who you are.

GEORGE: How do you hang on to what you are so that you won't become what you hate though?

CONSCIENCE: I would ask, how do you hang on to what you don't know that you are so that you won't become what you don't know how to hate. *(George does not respond)* Maybe by letting your conscience translate for you your next action into something that is compatible with your principles.

GEORGE: I don't know if I can stand constantly feeling your heavy steps ceaselessly running up and down my chest while shielding my own self from my next decision.

CONSCIENCE: It's not what you think.

GEORGE: Why do you say that? Is it not restrictive? Doesn't it restrict a person's freedom? Doesn't it…

CONSCIENCE *(Interrupting him)*: Quite the opposite. When you know what you believe in, when you are completely synchronized with your conscience, you feel an uncanny, powerful sense of freedom because you feel that you know yourself, and when you know the materials you are made of, you feel certain that you can rely on them. You know your strengths and, more importantly, you know your weaknesses. Consequently, you can see the road before you more clearly. It cannot hide its obstacles behind your own doubts, its deep cracks beneath your own misgivings. A person cannot get through the fog in front of him if first he does not get past the fog he sees when he looks inside him. That internal fog, the one that lives within every person is the one that determines not only where he will go, but also when he will stop.

GEORGE: Okay. So, are you saying that a person is defined by the size of his internal fog?

CONSCIENCE: I am saying that a person is defined by the fog he himself has created inside him to avoid seeing the part of himself he fears the most. As a result, it is easier for him to convince himself that this part does not belong to him, is not his and, therefore, he is not responsible for anything this part of his creates in the world around him.

GEORGE: But can you speak, even for a moment, to your next decision without being tempted to ask it what it wants from you?

CONSCIENCE: You know, every future decision of ours has long since planted a piece of itself inside us. The more important it is, the deeper it has sown.

GEORGE: You mean the future has long been living silently inside me, until its turn to become the present comes?

CONSCIENCE *(Gets up, goes to him, takes him by the hand and leads him to the small desk nearby where she takes a blank sheet of paper out of a drawer and sits him in front of it):* Introduce yourself to this gentleman. On this blank sheet of paper, in its emptiness which, if you look closely, is less white and less blank than what you think, but more voracious that anything you've seen in your life, live all your future decisions, all your mistakes, all your triumphs. Sit before it and find the courage to write down on its front side all that you hope for, and on its back side all that you fear. Next to each hope of yours write in parenthesis the character flaw you have to overcome to realize it, and next to each fear of yours write in parenthesis which virtue of yours you must mobilize to overcome it.

When you are done, you will have managed to make any fog that lives inside you take a step back and allow you to see better who you really are. When you realize what is hidden inside an unwritten truth, a truth which, though it belongs to you, has yet to find the courage to tell you her name, you will inevitably encounter, or rather you will be forced to traverse the deafening silence that lives permanently inside her, the most cruel silence there is, until you reach the part of your soul where, if you can stand to stay for a while talking about your feelings, you will be able to hear her speak for the first time in your life. This is the most precious truth in the world, the one truth that has managed to fit inside her all that connects your every decision, your every action, with you.

GEORGE: What are you saying? That the next actions of my life have long since lived inside me?

CONSCIENCE: That's right; they were born long ago, brought to life, without asking you, by your truth in a spot inside you only she knows.

GEORGE: And what about luck, does it play any role in this? Do you doubt, damn you, that a man's life is a product of luck?

CONSCIENCE: No, no, you're right; every person is a product of their luck. What could I say to someone who is simply waiting at a bus stop along with twenty other people and a car crashes into them killing only him?

GEORGE *(Thinks about it, as if wanting to change the focus of his argument)*: You might be right. You know, an elderly truth once told me: "Make your luck out of the part of yourself you know better than any other, regardless of how small it is". I followed her advice, and every day since then I have been trying to raise this part as best I can, like a diligent nanny who takes good care of a child that is not her own so that one day it will grow to become a decent person.

CONSCIENCE: I find it very interesting that you believe that your truth does not belong to you.

GEORGE *(Gets up, takes his chair and moves it a few feet further away and then sits down on it)*: I am not that arrogant.

CONSCIENCE: I am glad. You personally must become the wind that will clear away the fog you see each time when, staring at a blank page, you end up staring at yourself. I am talking about the fog that does its best to conceal from you parts of your own strength, especially your most important virtues and certainly some of your character flaws. How will you be able to produce a correct decision when you don't even know which tools, what parts of yourself, you have at your disposal? It is then that you yourself invite luck to infiltrate your next decision like a Trojan horse and shape it anyway she wants.

GEORGE: There is no doubt that luck has played a major role in my life, but don't you agree that the less we know about ourselves, the easier we surrender our future to her, a decision, an action at a time, so she can shape it anyway she wants?

CONSCIENCE: Don't underestimate yourself. You are not weak. You have vast reserves of strength in you, so long as you can find the key to unlock this fog that's doing all it can to hide you from what you are. You can defeat any opponent in your life, as long as you understand what he is made of, what his strengths and his weaknesses are made of. You are the product of your own self-awareness, made from the materials you provided her yourself. The better you know yourself and the material you are made of, the better you can control the considerable influence luck exerts on you anyway. How can a captain tell if his small boat will withstand the pounding waves if he doesn't know what materials it's made of? Are cardboard and steel equally strong? Make sure you know what material you are made of before you go out to sea, a sea that the wind rules with an iron hand, at times letting her stay calm, an endless cheerful serenity, and other times heaving all his strength at her, forcing her to bring forth from deep in her bowels devastating storms that can obliterate anything human made she finds in her path. A strong boat will withstand both, a weak one just the former. That's why you often see people who refuse to do the hard, arduous work required to find out who they really are, having made the wrong decision, they end up blaming luck for what happened to them.

GEORGE: I wish I had your confidence. I, on the other hand, feel as if every morning I get out of bed leaving behind me hundreds of decisions that won't find the strength to start constructing themselves using the tools I gave them the night before. I try to fool myself by thinking that the fact that I believe so much in my luck absolves me from the heavy, almost unbearable obligation of having to constantly become better, or even from the obligation to my self-esteem to try to get to know myself better than I already do. I don't know, maybe I am destined to constantly dance arm in arm with the sea of fogs made out of the parts of myself I will never be able to understand, the parts it might not suit my ego for me to know as well as I should.

CONSCIENCE: It's incredible how much man wants to know about everyone else and how little about himself.

GEORGE: Because you don't have to sweat, you don't have to hurt to learn something about someone else.

CONSCIENCE: Why, though, should you surrender your future to luck without a fight? What else does a man have besides his future?

GEORGE: Because he doesn't know how to manage himself, while it's far easier to pretend that he can manage others. Why don't you ask me for that matter? I have fought so many battles with luck, during which she never stopped trying to discover the mistakes I have managed to personally hide deep inside me so that my self-confidence won't find them.

CONSCIENCE: You mean those mistakes of yours behind which your good qualities are running, trying to discover them before they accidentally stumble on your shortcomings?

GEORGE: You mean to tell me that you don't know that a man's character flaws are much better at finding the mistakes he has already made faster than his good qualities can? Come on now!

CONSCIENCE: There is no greater pleasure for someone's luck than to discover how to have fun playing with the new man-toy which she just bought from the shop of his own self-awareness. It's the shop that his self-awareness opens after every major defeat of his on the sidewalk across from his logic, across from that spot where his greatest triumph wants to live. She does it just to be able to sell back to him the parts of his mind that he himself had thrown into the trash long ago, after another fight with his self-criticism which he had lost. The only thing left for him to do now is to hide behind his ablest delusion, so that he is unable to see his mistakes which have sat down a bit further on, and plead with him to come closer to them so that he may pick the one he wants to make.

GEORGE: I know, you have told me before: zero was discovered the first time man was able, in the most fearful part of his mind, to multiply the kind of truth he had plenty of with the kind of luck he had almost run out of. *(Pause)* Could it have been discovered when man first realized that his self-awareness didn't know as much about him as she had claimed that she did?

CONSCIENCE: Do you think it's possible that man leaves for work in the morning holding a deck of cards, each of which, instead of numbers and symbols, is marked with one of his shortcomings, written in big golden letters, which he uses throughout the day to divine where he hid the night before the part of his self-awareness which luck still allows him to use?

GEORGE: I sometimes wonder if my mistakes have an expiration date. I constantly feel them haunting me, or is it just one, which is constantly mutating and showing up each time wearing a different mask, a new facade, trying to play me, to have fun seeing me totally bewildered? How do my damn mistakes manage to be so much more cunning than me?

CONSCIENCE: They didn't become more cunning on their own, you made them like that. They know you so well because it was the dark side of your self-awareness that gave birth to them, the side you chose never to shed light on so you won't be terrified realizing who you are. And the worst part is that your own mistakes don't make mistakes. They will never make mistakes unless you get in between them and yourself confidence.

GEORGE: Unfortunately, that's the way things are ... Every time we have this conversation, I feel after a while as if the most defective part of myself wants to get out of my body, take a step forward, kneel down and ask my forgiveness.

(Pause) You devil, you are really enjoying this, standing across from me and proving, just by staring at me, how much stronger than me you are!

CONSCIENCE: Come here, let me tell you something. *(George gets up and goes to her, like a schoolboy who's been called to the blackboard by the teacher)* I have been watching you fight with yourself all this time, blaming your misery on everybody else except you. How convenient! Don't forget, it's not darkness that turns off the lights in your life, it's your sadness that does it. All these years, every time you look around you and can't figure out why you are unhappy, you send your mind to quickly fabricate as many excuses as you can, so that you won't find yourself face to face with the real reasons you feel miserable. It's so convenient for a soul to feel no need to do something to solve any problem when it's almost always someone else's fault!

The greatest enemy of your happiness is not anything bad that might happen to you, but all that you demand from her to get for you without you having anything to offer to her in return. Before you look around to find out why you are unhappy, lower your head and take a long look inside you. Search to find the abyss that managed to hide, and now permanently live in the part of your body you can illuminate less than any other with your logic, and try to pull it out so you can see its true dimensions. You see, those attributes of yours that want to have fun with you by occasionally making your life more difficult than it actually is, have this unique ability to produce their own twilight so as to appear to be much bigger than their actual size.

GEORGE: You're right, you're right. Every time I get into a fight with someone I feel as if I bend down as deep as I can inside me and, stretching my left arm until it almost pops out of its socket, I try to grab the abyss that lives inside me and pull it out, being as careful as I can not to damage its sensitive edges. I then wrap it around my soul and squeeze her with all my strength so she hurts so much that I can see myself being more miserable even than my most ambitious sorrow. How easy it is for a man, without any preparation, to instantly find the biggest ugliness hidden inside him and pull it out to show it off to the world around him. I've become so good at that! *(Seemingly relieved by what he just managed to say, as if a great weight was lifted from him)* I feel ready, I am ready to grab all the strength I have in me, regardless of how strong it is, and dragging it behind me march towards the highest wall of my soul, stand in front of it and try to tear it out, get it out of my body and bring it to you, so you can help me break it down. *(Pause)* But what kind of sledgehammer does one use to knock down such a wall, a wall made from the kind of thoughts that demand to have in them more cleverness than truth?

CONSCIENCE: With compassion.

GEORGE *(Fearing that this would be the answer but hoping that he could avoid hearing it, he turns his head away, as if wanting to quickly look at someone far away, so he won't be forced to look up close and stumble on his own self):* Can I stand, though, to live my life as the penniless tenant of my happiness, a man struggling at the end of each month to pay the rent for an apartment that will never be his own, or as the rich owner of my sorrow, a man who constantly lives far from any insecurity about how he will safeguard what he feels, paying the price of having to constantly live immobilized in the certainty that his permanent sorrow so generously offers him?

CONSCIENCE Is it time, perhaps, for you to adapt your soul to the quantity of kindness she can hold inside her?

GEORGE: Is it time, perhaps, for me to openly admit to my ego how much loneliness I want to have, or rather I can stand in my life?

CONSCIENCE *(Sits back down in her chair):* Maybe it's time for you to adjust your head to the dreams it can dream?

GEORGE: Is it time, perhaps, for me every morning, as soon as I wake up, not to open the back door of my body so that my shadow can get out and take, ahead of me, the first step I would take that day?

CONSCIENCE: Maybe it's time for you to ask the filthy rich beggar in your life, namely the time you have left, to give you another chance to get to know him all over again.

GEORGE: I might ask my delusions to give me another chance to get to know myself from the beginning.

CONSCIENCE: You mean for the first time?

GEORGE: Maybe… sort of… *(He lowers his head and turns it to the right and left, as if trying to find something he lost in his own body)* Damn me, I feel as if I have no more light in me to better illuminate the words I want to say, as if I don't have any extra soul in me to construct them properly. I want so much to believe that behind all these words running around like mad at the edge of my lips, jostling each other for position so I can see them better and pick them to represent me, there are, deeper inside me, other words, more timid, less handsome, which are, nonetheless, more solid, more honest, more precious.

CONSCIENCE: Precious to you or to the verbal argument you are struggling to formulate?

GEORGE: The...

CONSCIENCE *(Interrupting him):* How can you frame an argument to which, before you even start, you have given the ability to define you as a man?

GEORGE: The same way, or rather as easily as not being able to construct something you won't know how to demolish afterwards. Stop asking questions you know the answer to, because that way you are revealing that you don't know what you really want to ask. *(Pause)* You know that these are the words I want, the words I need right now to help me convey to you, not the beauty or the ugliness of what I am, but its very truth. *(He takes a step sideways while reaching out with his left hand, as if trying to show her something)* There, look, just a few hours ago I gave birth to these infant meannesses and now I am teaching them how to walk inside me before I let them free to gallop away astride the worker-words, those totally neutral words which any man who can no longer sustain any kindness in him fashions out of the strongest material he has, so they can stand to carry the unbearable weight of his apathy out of his mind.

CONSCIENCE: And, you know, the weight of a word carrying a lie on its back is many times greater than the weight of a word that is carrying a truth. These are the words that never wanted to express themselves, only to convey something. I feel as if each meanness I give birth to, before exiting my mouth, demands of me to show it where my truth is so it can try to rape her.

GEORGE: You mean to tell me that you feel like a rapist who tips his victim?

CONSCIENCE: Take it anyway you want.

GEORGE: I feel like a man who, to feel content, or rather to manage to get his hands on everything his ego always wanted to acquire, chose to rape his own truth rather than make love to his lie.

CONSCIENCE: I like what you just said, though I don't know if you too like it more than it disgusts you.

GEORGE: There are times when even my loneliness is bored with me and, leaving my side, makes me wonder, or rather makes me doubt whether my truth is strong enough to survive at the spot where my self-confidence is asking her to live, the spot in my life where my logic has chosen to no longer provide me with her services.

CONSCIENCE: Why, do you actually think that truth can survive beyond your mouth the edge of? You know that if you set up a table in the middle of your mind and sit across from yourself, after a few minutes, from various parts of your mind you would never expect, small packs of these thoughts of yours you never wanted to think about will come running, thoughts that always knew that they are not yours, always believed that you belong to them and not the other way around. If at that moment you manage to close your eyes and try to traverse the most bereft of meaning thought you've ever had in your life, you'll end up in a spot of your happiness where you will be able to overhear your most cherished hopes talk to each other, like seabirds of your soul that fly over your life's boat, waiting to dive and grab whichever leftovers of your sorrow you toss into its wake.

GEORGE: Are you actually asking me if I'm ready to get off at the next stop my life will make?

CONSCIENCE: No, don't start getting ready yet. You won't find that stop, it will find you. Besides, life doesn't have any stops, just lost opportunities that don't realize they are lost.

GEORGE: What do you mean?

CONSCIENCE: I mean a stop is not a stop if you can't get off.

GEORGE: Don't add to the pressure I am already under. You won't be the one to abolish sunshine from my life by deeming it illegal!

CONSCIENCE: It is I, though, who won't let you become the failed beggar of your past who, barely dressed in his most convincing outfit, the one that's more appropriately threadbare than all the others, goes out into the streets every morning asking anyone that passes before him if he has ever visited your past without you being present. He will keep searching all day long without stopping, until he finds the first person who will answer in the affirmative, whom he will then immediately beg for some of those charming smiles you once had, the ones that seemed as if they had just been brought to the surface of your life by the excavation of your most successful silence. How is it possible, as you get to know someone better, to realize how good his past is at not letting you find out anything more about him?

GEORGE: It's true, my past is better than me at hiding from any ambitious visitor those qualities of mine that always made me seem more giddy than unhappy, a man who always preferred to constantly have an unclean soul rather than a clear mind. Anyway, I am not afraid to admit that I always was a man who went around holding in my left hand a bucket full of dust which my soul liked me to use to cover any person that became close to me, to make him seem dirtier than me. So I always ended up convincing myself that I am cleaner than the people around me, though I knew that when all is said and done I was the dirtiest of them all.

CONSCIENCE: There is no one more unsatisfied, no one who will ever be able to find some serenity inside him that can stand living with him all the time, than a man who has forced himself to constantly fight in his life and, after winning, the first thing he does is to turn towards his victory to ask her how happy she will allow him to be.

GEORGE: Man, I feel like I can't breathe. So many yesterdays have gathered around us in the last few minutes. I feel their filthy hands pulling at my clothing like the rudest, most persistent beggars at a bazaar. They are so many that I can barely fit with them in my reality, which has been waiting for hours to take me by the hand and walk with me towards my next decision.

CONSCIENCE *(Gets up and pulls him to the window)*: Look outside, look at all the yesterdays you are talking about, look at them, they are all staring at you with eyes wide open, anxiously waiting for what you will say to them. If you look closely, in the middle of your greatest sorrow you will be able to see two young hopes of yours, they can't be more than a few days old, starting to perform their wedding ceremony on their own right now.

GEORGE: I, on the other hand, think that they are getting ready to commit suicide. I want so much to go and sit between these two hopes, to sit alone enwrapped in the oblivion of the dust that I manufacture myself to spread over the part of my life I really need to see less clearly. I want to talk to them, I want to hear what they don't want to tell me. By God, one of these days I will find the courage to break down the door of my beliefs to ask them why they won't let me stay emotionally suspended in mid-air for longer than necessary, be more passionate than what I was told is good for me, more insipid than the opinion of the people around me would like me to be, less impressive than my public image has been pushing me for years to become, a worse social climber than my status demands. And if the price is for me to become more transparent so that people can more easily understand what they see when they try to look inside me, so be it. How many more walls will I construct in my life, I wonder, to prevent the people I love from going to where my loneliness celebrates her victories every night arm in arm with her favourite spoils? It's the ones which, since she wasn't able during the day to persuade my happiness to hand them over to her, she always ended up, shortly before midnight decreed her end, assaulting her to steal them from her. How many more moats must I build around my heart to prevent anyone from getting inside me except for those who have managed to steal the password of her main gate?

CONSCIENCE: And once they manage to open the main gate of your heart, what makes you so sure that they will find what they hoped for inside?

GEORGE: I have no idea.

CONSCIENCE: The impasses which your awkwardness so cheerfully gives birth to really like to stay suspended in the thin yet mighty fog that lives between the ego of your stupidity and the moderation of your intelligence which, equally proud of both, you continue to enjoy.

GEORGE: I no longer know how many different kinds of kindness I have in me. I don't know how many are still willing to let me use them, so I can show the people around me what is left of what I am if I manage to temporarily disarm my meanness, removing even a single bullet from the gun which she installed herself long ago in the middle of my mouth. I don't know how many more flowers I can cut from the only field in my soul which doesn't allow my logic to dictate to her what she can plant. I want so much to give them to the sensual pleasure of the great rage that lives on the side of my life's mountaintop that is always dark, because the sun is afraid to send his rays there, since he knows that they will never come back alive. And he needs them, he doesn't have any others... I want so much to manage to persuade this cursed rage to stop coming down so often from where it lives, just so it can find me and make me hurt.

CONSCIENCE *(Jumps up suddenly and says more intensely):* Dam you, I can no longer stand listening to you dig to discover the spot which human logic must never try to reach, unless she is prepared to grab the heaviest wound she can carry in her hands and start smashing with it anything precious, anything vulnerable, anything defenseless the brain of her owner has in it!

GEORGE: Savouring the bitter aftertaste your words cheerfully leave on my serenity's shoreline, I realize that for days now I have been insistently asking the interpretation of my life to let me take a break from all the chores it has assigned to me, but the damn thing won't let me. It keeps me caged in the strength I became to satisfy my weakness, the success I became to satisfy my failure, the sorrow I became to satisfy my biggest sorrow, trapped between the mines which the brightest part of my self-criticism laid some truths ago, about midway to the only spot in every day which, even momentarily, has a view of the one truth in my life I was never able to understand, because every time I try to approach her to talk to her she ends up running away.

CONSCIENCE: She does that because you never found the courage to become a man who despises his shadow less than his own self.

GEORGE: Why, could you become someone who could be equally happy if you were forced to live with your view restricted to the backside of your life?

CONSCIENCE: I don't know. You see, we consciences don't easily agree to give birth to the dreams our owners want, especially when you push us hard to do it. And when we cannot, you end up using those damn middlemen.

GEORGE: What middlemen?

CONSCIENCE: You know, the middlemen, your chemical friends, all the substances you put inside you to help you run faster than you could run on your own, hoping you might escape who you are. I am talking about the middlemen you need to be able to start a conversation with your own soul. I never understood why you allow them to come sell you your very soul, always keeping a piece, the truest one, for themselves. Especially when, having no use for it, they take an indifferent, contemptuous look at it and then toss it into the trash.

GEORGE: You make me feel like something more than what I am able to realize that I am and something less than what I am afraid to realize I can become.

CONSCIENCE: At the starting line of your self-confidence you have hidden two cowardices which for years now have had something to tell you. Take a few steps back, turn around and listen to them!

GEORGE: Right now I don't even want to hear what the next sentence I've had in my mouth for quite some time wants to tell me!

CONSCIENCE: The one you put there yourself or the one I did? You know that, as long as you let yourself be the favorite toy of every word you utter, you won't be able to recognize what you really want to say in what you just said.

GEORGE: To answer you, I will first have to climb my mind's most ambitious peak and start running in the direction my most conscientious cowardice will point out to me.

CONSCIENCE: I am sure that each time you found it tough going in your life you always pretended that you lived in a reality next to the one you actually were in. Essentially, while permanently living in an ambiguity next to your least courageous decision, you managed to fool your self-confidence into believing that you are smarter than her.

GEORGE: What do you mean?

CONSCIENCE: Bring me the checkbook your soul used to write checks to your sorrow during the last month and you'll understand what I mean.

GEORGE: There are nights which, no matter how hard I tried, I never managed to emotion-proof well enough so as not to lose any feelings of mine I had put in them. These dam nights have managed to exorcise every last source of optimism off me by kicking them in the face, making me feel that my shortcomings, being more capable than me, have managed to build within my self-confidence a self-confidence of their own, which wants to attend to their needs before it deals with my own.

CONSCIENCE: A soul is missing for slavery to become hope.

GEORGE: Some minimal ambition might be missing from a curve to finally find the courage to stretch its body as much as it can and become a straight line.

CONSCIENCE: Why don't you ask the straight lines in your life that belong to you if they are willing to forget their beliefs, maybe even betray them, so that they may fall in love with the freedom contained in a curve that has the ability to give its body any shape it wants.

GEORGE: What makes you think that if straight lines had a choice about what shape they could have they wouldn't choose to be curves?

CONSCIENCE: Leave straight lines alone and talk to me about the one straight line in your life I care about.

GEORGE: Which one is that?

CONSCIENCE: Your self-confidence.

GEORGE: Okay, okay. I sometimes wonder how I managed to build a self-confidence by sticking together hundreds of my dreams, those dreams which, since I knew that I would never manage to find the courage to dream them, for years I ended up, before going to sleep every night, tossing them in advance just before midnight into the trashcan my normality brought me and left next to my bed stand. Why did I do that? Why? *(Starts walking nervously back and forth in the room)* Oh hope of mine unlock me from my memory, and unlock me not only from what I remember but also from what my pessimism insists on remembering.

Without being able to do anything to prevent it, I feel as if I have become my pessimism's most ardent fan, the man who rushes to close his ears each time he sees his truth approaching, waiting for his sorrow to translate for him a few minutes later what she just said to him using only the most cherished, the blackest, most dusty words she has. Thus I end up feeling imprisoned in the absolute freedom my cowardice has gained without my permission, in the ability she has, whenever she decides, to make me feel anyway she likes, instantly transforming me into a person who, to figure out what he feels, must first escape from what he owes himself to think about. How the hell did I end up feeling constantly obliged to ask my shortcomings if they agree with what I am about to say before I even utter a single word?

CONSCIENCE: Knowing you, perhaps even before you thought about it...

GEORGE: Perhaps... I am watching my logic which, wallowing in the mud of the ten words with which my ego from when I was eighteen never stopped being in love, struggles tooth and nail to save me, or rather to save what I am from what I show that I am.

CONSCIENCE: But...

GEORGE: *(Interrupting her abruptly)*: Why did I let you become the judge of my behavior, who demands to stay on duty round the clock inside me? It's as if I have installed a permanent traffic cop in my soul who sits on the edge of my lips and lets only the words he wants come out of my mouth. I feel as if I manage to give birth to my misery all over again each time I let this traffic cop order my soul to sit down like a schoolchild, pleading with my logic to answer the stainless steel questions that the reality in which my internal fog forces me to live wants to ask me.

These are the questions that demonstrate their satisfaction by smiling at me with an incredibly bitter smirk each time they pass in front of my mind and see it bleeding from its most vulnerable, its most moderate edge, the one that for years now I have left almost undefended because I never dared to find out how far from my normality it can stand to live. This damn edge has managed to convince me that it's worth more than all the other parts of my mind, because it is responsible for my survival, not like the others whose only care is to make me think about simple things that seduce my ego, having nothing to offer to tomorrow's reality which they bought on my behalf.

CONSCIENCE: It's not my fault, it's your malice that has this unique ability to transform you into what your melancholy always wanted you to be, a darkness that is proud of how much more black than any other it can fit in itself. It's this malice of yours that is able to persuade the infallible needs of your ego to start producing from scratch, one by one, each pulse of your heart that never tried to figure out how to beat the way it wanted to.

GEORGE: Have you ever seen a man who could, with a single breath, take such a deep dive into himself that he could reach the most ambitious hole he has in him? I can. I do it every time I let my hatred flood my life, every time I let it ride me, forcing me to walk for hours among those mines that have chosen to live scattered all over inside it, ordering me to step where it wants. It's this hole which, until it managed to teach me how to feel less strong, convinced me to be less optimistic, the one which, because it didn't know how to teach me to love, ended up showing me how to hate.

    As long as my past taps me on the shoulder, wanting to persuade me to confide in it, without anyone overhearing us, what the heading of my next melancholy will be before I even begin to experience it, I will continue to move along with my head tucked in the future, pretending that I do not see what I have already seen, pretending that I do not feel what I have already felt. Thus, I continue to devour my next happiness pretending that I have not already asked my logic to translate her to me into concepts my ego can bear to understand, while at the same time I do everything I can to avoid stumbling on those questions of my sorrow that would rather stay corroded than spotless, the ones which for quite some time now demand to confront, not me, but my defeatism.

CONSCIENCE: Ah, those corroded questions! The little devils, every time they make me run as fast as I can to grab by the throat any 'maybe' that's trying to escape the oversight of your self-confidence so I can bring it back and make it introduce itself for the thousandth time to your defeatism, I realize that your mind has already explicitly prohibited you from asking these questions, not because it is afraid that you might answer them, but because it hopes that it will never need to hate them as much as you do.

GEORGE: All these 'maybes' you refer to have been circling around my next decision for a few days now, bursting into laughter every time they manage to trip her up, before I have time to get her through into tomorrow safe and sound. The little devils have started an incredible dance seeing me take those five mid-air, perfectly blue steps to get my hands on that cursed book that has instructed every word written on its pages how to unbearably hurt the surface of my eyes when they try to read them. Every time I draw near that book, it has already managed to open my soul on any page it wants before I even get a chance to open it myself.

It's the book in between whose pages I have been discovering for years, every time I open it, one of those defective banknotes that my life is using to purchase me from my own time. I am talking about those banknotes of time that intentionally destroyed part of themselves so they can no longer depict their value and thus manage to prove to me what mine is. They have moved from where I placed them and are now between the pages that describe the exploits of my cowardice. They have all gone there to hide together, hoping I will never find the strength to read them. So I end up each time, as soon as I stumble upon them by mistake, running to hide, as fast as I can, between my two weakest qualities, hoping I'll avoid looking them in the eyes, giving them a chance to seduce me.

CONSCIENCE: I hope these pages don't coincide with those pages of your logic that...

GEORGE: Don't interrupt me... The dam book loves these banknotes more than its torn pages, the ones I tore so that I won't have to admit to myself that not only did I want to, but I could stomach reading them to the end. As time went by, I felt that this book began watching me from inside the bookcase, trying each time I wasn't looking, to slip by me hoping it would manage to put in my pockets those words that it fears so much, the ones that describe the way my next mistake will be born. I let them play with me, while I kept on hearing from the depths of my being the cry of the store display I show to the outside world calling out what it wants to believe it is selling.

My right hand trembles as it begins to realize that all the signatures of strength it stole from the thousands of hands I have shaken in my life are leaping out of my past, each one separately, to ask me to return to them the false promises I made them. Abruptly pulling every handshake of mine back to my hand and caressing it for a few seconds, I realize that I I've become one with all that I don't understand and, even worse, I've become one with what I won't let my logic realize that I fear. How the hell have I ended up believing that if I manage to mix up inside me the dreams midnight has about me and those I have about the coming day, I might begin to feel that I should no longer be ashamed to admit that I have become the accident of the one truth in my life that loves my ambiguity more than she loves me, an accident that demands to have one more question for me than those I can answer?

CONSCIENCE: I have some good news. I can see far away a minimal night unzipping the longest night you have seen in your life and jump from inside it to come meet us. The poor thing really wants to know how a night can be blacker for those people like you that haven't learned yet how to hope in a proper manner. She walks bravely by herself, and in a little while, without your protection, she will begin crossing the most disreputable neighbourhoods of your mind, using some of those old steps of yours that always knew how to proclaim to the people around you the bloody melody your internal fog sang each time it couldn't see by itself where it wanted to take you. The damn things have a way of letting you use them for a while so you can reach ahead of your sorrow that future of yours where, as soon as you set foot in it, you will order them to immediately start slashing you into a thousand pieces. It's those steps that will take hold of your body, nail it on themselves and force you to take for every step forward a thousand ones backward, to feel for every happy moment a thousand worries, until you come across the one that started it all.

GEORGE: I feel like the various extramarital affairs I have with my authenticity will soon all get together in the least ambitious part of my mouth to bid me goodbye. So what are you implying, that it's time I go meet them?

CONSCIENCE: Yes, right...I was always impressed by how many people don't realize that the darkest spot of their mouth is the most transparent part of their body, allowing the dozens of words waiting in its lobby to be clearly seen by the people they talk to. Some wait patiently, sitting in the back, others, quite anxious, walk nervously back and forth on the edge of their lips. The more one struggles to hide the contents of his mouth from the people around him, the more it becomes, in a ridiculous way, progressively more transparent, more visible.

GEORGE: Often in my life, while looking around, I saw the meanness that everyone had inside them feeling disappointed by their behavior and, exhausted, run to hide in the only hideout that would accept her, their deep past. I must thank all the people I met in my life who allowed me to feel their kindness. I am most grateful. Without knowing it, they did me a great favour, helping me, even for a short time, to discover what mine looked like! I would like to thank them for helping me realize, each time from scratch, that at the spot inside me where the limits of kindness have decided to erase themselves, a brand new misery demanded to be born right away every time. This is how I came to realize that each time I hated someone, the only thing I managed to do is to toss another little piece of darkness, not in his soul, but into mine. I keep forgetting that the unbearable pain felt by the meanness that exists in my self-confidence often makes her ask me, before I start letting my rage spill out to attempt to drown the souls of the people around me, to devote a few seconds to her so she can explain to me why I should hate them.

CONSCIENCE: That sneaky devil is even more effective than the meanness of your loneliness.

GEORGE: Yes, she is…

CONSCIENCE: You can't hate someone before you try to find out why you hate him.

GEORGE: Everytime I am in pain… *(His eyes fill with tears)* Everytime my soul is in pain and demands to spill her toxic fluid all around her to make others hurt even more than she does, I feel that every next step of mine makes me feel shorter, removing an inch, a pride, a whole section of who I am at that moment.

CONSCIENCE *(Interrupting him)*: Isn't that what sorrow is? The realization that through his actions a person proves to himself that he is something less than what he could have been? Isn't that what sorrow is all about? The realization that his own actions are pushing him to not respect himself?

GEORGE: How did I end up drifting around in my own life, holding in my right hand my meanness' huge saber, which I whirl over the head of any sunbeam that believes that its reason for existence is to make the life of the people around me brighter, happier? This way I become that day in February which believes more than any other in winter's splendor, a beautiful sorrow that is no longer happy just feeling sorry for herself, but wants to spread the ugliness of her beauty all around her, trying every minute of her life to cover everything she sees before her with the most invisible, unbearably heavy burden there is in the world.

CONSCIENCE: That's right. Every ugliness is a beauty that never learned how to be content with what she is. So, I am really glad to hear that you no longer believe in this stupid theory that by making people around you hurt, the pain you feel inside you is magically transferred to them, making the spot that gave birth to it not hurt at all after a while. I am sorry though that you feel that every minute you live you must compare yourself to the best man you could be right then. What an unbearable burden!

GEORGE: Especially when you don't believe that it is you who is carrying it.

CONSCIENCE: Who is carrying it?

GEORGE: Your delusions.

CONSCIENCE: Interesting. Which part of your mind, I wonder, can survive between your delusions and your perfectionism?

GEORGE: I don't know, perhaps the part that hasn't realized yet that it's not necessary for a man to be sad to feel fully alive.

CONSCIENCE: It is necessary, however, for a person first to learn how to be sad in order to learn how to live.

GEORGE: Let me tell you. I gain so much strength, so much energy when I see every bullet from the gun of my meanness, every toxic word I utter, forget the reason it was fired from the barrel of the machinegun that lives constantly with the safety off in the middle of my mouth and, defying the orders of the anger that spawned it, decide on its own to drop to the earth before it hits its target. I see many people that I socialize with, while we are talking, get ambushed by thousands of bullets, bullets similar to mine, bullets that started their life burdened with as much pain and meanness as their owners could fit into each one of them. They had the foresight to let the kindness they encountered in their path strip them of the anger they had in them and persuade them to drop to the ground before they started destroying the target they were meant to hit.

CONSCIENCE: You should know that the soil of your authenticity is the only one that can bear both your weight and the weight of your lies. It's the only one that can welcome you when you don't know where else to go to be able to keep standing upright. Relieved as you are from the enormous burden that your rage makes you constantly carry on your back, that smile from way back, which for years you had lost, comes back to join you again after a long absence. Tell me that you have felt it, tell me... Tell me that when you're standing on this soil you feel the earth beneath you tremble, not out of fear but out of optimism, wanting to bring forth from within it and give to you as a gift a more serene tomorrow, a future that will be made of days that have only one night in them. Maybe then you will manage to understand what two consecutive midnights confided to you long ago: "When you stop hurting inside you will stop hating, and when you stop hating, you will stop shooting".

GEORGE: Yes, that's right.

CONSCIENCE: Do you realize that in every bullet, verbal or actual, that you fire, instead of gunpowder you have put a piece of yourself inside it? Usually it is not any piece but the one that hurts most of all at that moment.

GEORGE: What I can't overcome, because I can no longer understand it unless I manage to strip it completely by taking off the very last of the protection it is wearing, is that part of my anger that constantly avoids me. It's the one I have ended up fearing even more than my smartest meanness, the meanness that knows how to hide in the back side of my ego, where everything that is real refuses to be understood before it becomes completely transparent.

CONSCIENCE: Why don't you try to stop being fascinated by the truths you have produced yourself by realities you're doing your best not to find out what they contain, so you won't feel obliged to defend them if in the course of your life they prove to be less real than you thought?

GEORGE: I really wish I were able to figure out which good quality of mine is the one that enjoys so much making me feel more incompetent and more useless than any of my shortcomings!

CONSCIENCE: The answer to the previous question was just born in the one that followed.

GEORGE: What do you mean?

CONSCIENCE: Who gives birth to your victories and your defeats?

GEORGE *(Pause)*: My kindness and my meanness, I think.

CONSCIENCE: And who gives birth to your kindness and your meanness?

GEORGE: The darkness that lives in that fog I cannot see but can only feel. I see it in me. I get more anxious about my step after next rather than about the next one. I panic when I can't see on which of my shortcomings I am stepping on to take a step forward, and even more when I am forced to not step on any of my good qualities to manage it, every time I see life before me covered in that horrible invisible darkness borne of this hideous delusion, the one that owes itself to be first a witch and then a fog.

CONSCIENCE: It's the one that really likes, before you let your body get into your next step, to have already forced you to gamble your logic at craps, not to see what you might win, but to see what you will lose. Thus, in an instant, without realizing it, you transform yourself into an uncontrollable aggressive being, into a machine producing endless rage which, to survive, thinks only of itself and instinctively attacks, without being able to realize the reason it is doing so. You no longer even know how to win, you no longer know if you want to defeat the darknesses that don't want to defeat you, the ones that simply insist on constantly living a fearful breath next to you, ceaselessly judging you. *(Pause)* You don't even know how to switch on the light hoping that you might be able to scare them. It is an emotionally unbearable moment when a man realizes for the first time that he knows how to switch off any darkness in his life but, no matter how hard he tries, he will never manage to learn how to switch off even the smallest darkness that lives inside him.

GEORGE: I wish I knew that too. I wish I had tried harder to learn how to do that. *(Pause)* How though?

CONSCIENCE: By smiling at it.

GEORGE: Perhaps.

CONSCIENCE: I think by showing it that you are stronger than it.

GEORGE: How, though, can you persuade a darkness to fight with you?

CONSCIENCE: Only by persuading it to get into the wrestling ring of your truth.

GEORGE: To fight with my truth or with me?

CONSCIENCE: Who told you that whenever a man fights with somebody else he is not fighting with his own truth at the same time?

GEORGE: I don't know... I wish I could feel like that too, I wish my soul could persuade the darkness, any darkness, even the smallest one, to do something for her. I am afraid that I simply don't have the ability... I might have had it once, but not any longer.

CONSCIENCE: What a shame that today's souls don't know the footnotes that the past wants to put on the history that tomorrow intends to write about them.

GEORGE: That is true if you believe that there is a part of tomorrow that is not made just out of future.

CONSCIENCE: What are you asking me? If I believe that there is a tomorrow that doesn't want to show you all its parts?

GEORGE: No, if you believe that a part of tomorrow, the most devious one, the most difficult to defeat, has already started today making its most cowardly self inside me.

CONSCIENCE: Using what as building materials?

GEORGE: Probably whatever it finds looking through those parts of my heart I hid as deep as I could in the wake left by my apathy as it passed through my serenity.

CONSCIENCE: Choose one of the fairytales which your ego likes to grab from inside the consciences of the people around you to play with them until it makes them seem like the latest model of its truth, and then come back to continue our discussion.

GEORGE: Should I first stop explaining to my imagination the hopes I once had for her?

CONSCIENCE: Why do you involve your imagination in a discussion that has to do with yesterday?

GEORGE: Why, from where do you think a man's imagination draws all its strength?

CONSCIENCE: If you want to take the conversation there, why don't you try sitting next to those moments of old which refuse to open their curtains to show you what lies behind them, the side of your past you always wanted but never managed to make truly yours? They keep them shut because time enjoys watching you agonize while you reminisce about your past without having anything positive to say about it.

GEORGE: You mean those moments from a man's past which, because he never managed to conquer them, to make them his, the damn things have managed to insinuate themselves ahead of him into every moment in his future which he will try to grab himself from the hands of the neutrality, the detachment that lives in his boredom, hoping that this way he will manage to turn it into happiness?

CONSCIENCE: Yes, exactly.

GEORGE: The impasses which my awkwardness so happily gives birth to really like to drift in between the various 'maybes' that exist around me, the ones that live between my ego and my stupidity which, equally proud of both, I keep carrying with me wherever I go.

CONSCIENCE: Since you mentioned your boredom, time roars with laughter seeing the quantity of boredom it managed to put in the two totally empty hours it just gave you as a gift. It gave them to you to see what a person who hates his time as much as you can do with them.

GEORGE: But...

CONSCIENCE: It enjoys watching you trying to find a quick way to invent different excuses and so manage to refuse to taste the honesty the next minutes of your life hide inside them, because you know that a conscience that has decided to wake up after a long time again can become dangerous. The melancholy you have so skilfully hidden in the pleasant moments you so thoughtlessly continue to give away to your vanity is ready to direct the exchange of the colorless emotions with any part of your soul that never believed the version of truth which all these years now you have forced it to carry on your behalf inside it. The damn thing managed to fill every last cubic foot of the room you live in with the deadly gas that only kills emotions, leaving any argument it finds in front of it, which your logic has constructed on her own, untouched.

As it moves it is trying, with all the means at its disposal, to neutralize all the precious oxygen your soul breathes, to force you to get to the point where you can't breathe in what you really feel. *(She turns her back on him and goes to the end of the room)* Are you ready to accept into your body again your two hearts, especially the second one, the one that you always used to enable yourself to feel any emotion that the first one was afraid to feel? You used to have the courage, the stamina to wear them both in your body at the same time, but now the only thing you can do is to keep on hoping that soon they will agree to come out of the alibi your self-awareness uses to make you feel less like an illegal immigrant in your own life than what you already are and ask you to allow them to get to know you all over again.

GEORGE: I don't know…

CONSCIENCE: What do you mean "I don't know"? I am sure that you do know, however, how many self-expiring feelings of guilt you now manage to fit in the last glance the mirror gives you at night before you go to sleep.

GEORGE: I don't even know how many fit in the last glance winter gives me before he transforms his most pessimistic part into the fist which in the middle of February he will crawl by himself till he reaches spring to handover, not directly to it, but to its optimism. Poor winter does all that knowing that spring will use this fist a few days later to knock him down, to defeat him once and for all.

CONSCIENCE: Yes, indeed, at the dawn of its first day, spring cuts the ribbon for the grand opening of the least obscure and most beautiful optimism there is in the world.

GEORGE *(An intense sunbeam comes through the window and lights up the middle of the room)*: Quiet…Look, look at the edge of the sunbeam's body. Look, look how it bleeds joy from inside it.

CONSCIENCE: Even the greatest joy in the world can only fit one new sunbeam in it at a time.

GEORGE: Even the biggest cemetery in the world can only fit one new tear in it at a time.

CONSCIENCE: You say that because you were in such a hurry to find out how to be unhappy before you hear that word for which your joy chased after you for years trying to confide it to you, before you figure out how to buy from your melancholy at the end of each day all those gifts you always wanted to give to your joy. I wish you were normally half as clever as when you're unhappy!

GEORGE: You're right. I discovered this years ago. I am so much better at finding reasons to be miserable than at finding reasons to be cheerful.

CONSCIENCE: What a shame that man has the ability to become smarter the sadder he wants to feel!

GEORGE *(Turns around, takes a chair and sets it down as far from his conscience as he can)*: But what am I saying. I know how much I always liked to live in my handmade darknesses, the ones which since my childhood I sat making for hours piece by piece by myself so I could trust them when I would later need them, knowing how well made they were.

CONSCIENCE: I am not convinced. It's wasn't you who made your present sorrow. It was carefully manufactured by the one word which for days now always finds a novel and miraculous way to shipwreck a few seconds before you think it up in the harbor of your mind, where you are trying to offload as big a part of your beliefs as you can on the next word you will utter. *(Pause)* I have already explained this to you before. If you want to learn how to properly be sorry let a spring day, any spring day, show you.

GEORGE: A spring day?

CONSCIENCE: Yes. Who better knows sorrow than the greatest joy? Who better knows the most devastating gale than absolute calmness? Who better knows the most impenetrable darkness than the sun? Don't forget that your sorrow is so good at selecting on her own, without asking you, the spot inside you where she will place every emotion you allow to touch you. She can quickly dive to find in the deepest part of your abyss your most timid, your most secret sensitivity, the one you keep hidden in the lowest drawers of your soul, because you feel so embarrassed whenever you are all alone beside her, like someone in love who doesn't know how to behave the first time he meets his loved one. It is these feelings you have hidden in that place because you want to be sure that when you need them you will know exactly where they are.

GEORGE: Yes, yes... Holding the key made from her own body, she comes and opens any door of my soul I keep deliberately closed, not because I am scared of what I might find once I open it, but because I am scared about which of the parts of myself I pretend I can still understand, I have hidden in a spot of hers I will never find again. I am not afraid of the strength of whatever I have hidden in her, but of my weakness, my inability to bear to look it in the eyes.

CONSCIENCE: Should I tell you how I managed, without you seeing me, to throw another darkness in the well of your memory?

GEORGE: No.

CONSCIENCE: Why not? Come on, you know that we consciences are the favorite choreographers of the silence you like to use as a shield in front of your mouth to protect yourselves from that side of your logic you cannot figure out what she is trying to hide from you everytime you try to talk to her, the side you don't know how to refuse to grant any favor she asks for before you let her vanquish you with her charm.

GEORGE: Sometimes I wonder what would happen if my silence learned how to lie.

CONSCIENCE: You would become the truth of your shadow.

GEORGE: The what?

CONSCIENCE: The truth which your shadow has hidden in that spot of hers where you will most certainly look first when you decide to find out which part of your happiness you have hidden inside her.

GEORGE: I wouldn't want to… I don't know if I could ever do that…

CONSCIENCE: In your place I would wonder what will happen if your silence finds out what you really want to say!

GEORGE: That could be the intelligence of a silence.

CONSCIENCE: No, that's her racism.

GEORGE: What do you mean?

CONSCIENCE: I mean that when man produces a silence, he is always under the impression that he is smarter than her. What a delusion!

GEORGE: I don't understand.

CONSCIENCE: Have you never felt that from the moment she's born a silence you just created already considers you her inferior?

GEORGE: What are you saying, that man is a victim of his own silence?

CONSCIENCE: No, it's not man who is the victim of his own silence but his honesty. If you want to be sure, ask yourself the five most important questions your honesty refuses to answer and you will see that your silence hides behind all five of them.

GEORGE: Don't...

CONSCIENCE: Do you know that towards the end of his life, man feels the need to invite all the silences he ever made but never used?

GEORGE: Hold on a second, what did he do with them all these years, where did he store them?

CONSCIENCE: Let me finish. He invites them to get to know them better, some to give them a chance to know him from the beginning, some maybe even for the first time. He does not want to leave this world without getting to know who he could have been if he had allowed himself to say the last word, the one word which if he had uttered it during every fight he had in the past it would have managed to alter the course of his life thereafter, the one word which, after every time he made love, he kept inside him, imprisoned behind the iron bars of his greatest shame, the one word he didn't allow his lips to shape until they made it seem like a kindness every time he came face to face with the meanness all around him. *(Pause)* How different his life would have been if he had been able to remove from each time he quarreled with someone the one word that always insisted on being the toxic headline of all he said!

GEORGE: Wow, I can't even imagine what mine would be! You mean to say that a silence of mine could be living inside me all these years without me having ever felt her presence?

CONSCIENCE: I am afraid so. Not only that, but these are the silences that carry the most pain inside them.

GEORGE: Why?

CONSCIENCE: Because they don't know how to hurt others.

GEORGE: But...

CONSCIENCE: It's incredible how you humans learn from an early age to be such good opponents of your happiness!

GEORGE: Yes, each one of us is so good at constantly inventing new ways to defeat her.

CONSCIENCE: Which sometimes are so original...

GEORGE: The taste of truth I feel in my mouth right now is so incredibly sweet and sour, so incredibly expensive. I don't know if I can stand it. I feel the taste of what you just told me come and leave in the middle of my mind a lie that is so beautiful that it has long believed it is not actually fake.

CONSCIENCE: Beware of those gifts your shadow generously gives you. Don't pick them up if you don't know what's inside them.

GEORGE: Don't worry. The sewers that run on the right and left in my mind are filled with such gifts.

CONSCIENCE: What makes you so sure that only you have the right to toss whatever is no longer useful to you in to the sewers of your mind?

GEORGE: Who else could do it?

CONSCIENCE: I could, for instance.

GEORGE: But... *(Becomes extremely embarrassed)*

CONSCIENCE: You should know that in a city's sewers you can find many more leftovers of guilt that human waste. And wait till you see what's happening in the sewers of your mind!

GEORGE: Strolling among your words I feel as if I am crossing a graveyard of thoughts that demands to be both emotionally infinite and intellectually minimal, a graveyard whose surface consists of an intensely yellow toxic soil which, the moment I step on it, transforms into a gorgeous gentle red.

CONSCIENCE: In this graveyard, have the people buried their thoughts or have the thoughts buried their owners?

GEORGE: Why should I clarify that?

CONSCIENCE: So that...

GEORGE *(Interrupting her)*: Let a mental misstep obtain the alibi it deserves to have.

CONSCIENCE: Okay, so be it.

GEORGE: So, wherever I turn to look, I see human figures I met in my life who have a truth hanging around their neck which never sought to find out how truthful she is. They are all nervously looking right and left trying to figure out why they think that they owe so much to each other, why they all have to live deeply in debt to what each one's intelligence demands of him. By God, I could never figure out what this dam truth wanted to tell me!

CONSCIENCE: Did you want to know?

GEORGE: I was never sure...

CONSCIENCE: These truths are the dreams you never dared to dream. And so, your truth ends up transforming every lonely road she sees before you into a steep downhill, a downhill which, because it refuses to let even a little optimism shed light on it, is so blindingly bright, a downhill which, because you can see much more than you can understand, you end up unable to recognize anything, a downhill that won't even let you see where you have already been, because it knows that for your own good it must do its best to conceal it from you. It has already sown on its own throughout its length thousands of rusty nails that impatiently wait open-mouthed to shred your bare feet into as many pieces as they can.

GEORGE: It isn't the truth, it is you, my favorite conscience, who joyfully takes out of your pockets these thousands of rusty nails you speak of and spreads them all around my next day, then takes off my shoes and takes me by the hand to make me walk through it. It is you, I know it, I know…

CONSCIENCE: Don't let the darkness of your sorrow light up the only road in your life you can cross without the help of your guilt.

GEORGE: What do you mean?

CONSCIENCE: Let me get you across to the opposite shore of your own intelligence, let me help you find what you forgot to forget, what you left to your past long ago to keep an eye on, ever since your stupidity was always eager to buy any piece of your future that your self-awareness was inclined to sell her.

GEORGE: Stop, I'm not ready yet to take back the part of my joy I gave my shadow to watch over. I am not ready to feel this incredibly inarticulate nakedness that seeks to burst out of any darkness in my life I refuse to realize is not as dark as I would like and spill all over my mind's most peaceful neighbourhoods to enslave them with its seductive power. Please. No more words, no more marathon negotiations with white, no more exchanges of trophies with every guilt of mine that wants to shape my happiness anyway she wants, no more promises of stunning free falls, especially those that since long ago I have exclusively dedicated to my cowardice.

CONSCIENCE: You're right. Every free fall seems incredibly appealing seconds before you fall.

GEORGE: You know, I can no longer stand every time to let my most talented lie buy me off my sorrow one minute before I open the door to my soul so I can personally introduce myself to what I am trying to sell her.

CONSCIENCE: Not even the serenity you borrow from the look of any person that hurt you in your life. Blurry is the store display of a soul that doesn't know what she's selling.

GEORGE: I don't borrow it, I steal it. *(Pause)* If I weren't so good at being kind, I would be smarter.

CONSCIENCE: If you weren't smarter, you'd be happier.

GEORGE: I feel that my freedom today is ready to declare bankruptcy.

CONSCIENCE: Stop her. Become her favorite banknote. Help her settle the debt she owes to your smile. Become useful in what your memory doesn't wish to remember so she won't be forced to insult your future before you are forced to insult it yourself.

GEORGE: I don't understand what she's asking me to do. To buy myself from my sorrow?

CONSCIENCE: Let me tell you. Don't you see me, every time you are ready to say something important, run like crazy holding a big mirror in my hands to be in time to set it up at the entrance of your mind so that your words are able, before venturing out, to look at themselves even for a few seconds. I am doing the best I can to make them see so they can fully realize who they really are, with how much ugliness you have dressed each one of them, so they can see the enormous burden you have made them carry on their backs. And you know, the weight of ugliness is often much heavier that the weight of truth.

    I am the mirror who doesn't have a shiny surface like all others, but a surface on which you can rest your gaze for a while and, after you leave me alone for a moment or two to process it, I'll give it back to you a little later clean, based on what I think clean means, cleansed of this cursed dust in your life that has settled all over it. I am the mirror that enables you to communicate with those parts within you that you can no longer clearly see on your own.

GEORGE: You sly fox, you once again managed to tie me up with this incredibly crafty, invisible rope, which consciences like to use to tie up every spring day which lives in the spot of their owner's heart that logic has intentionally left unguarded. They say that consciences are the most dangerous terrorists in the world, and they are probably right.

CONSCIENCE: Only the consciences of those people who choose to constantly live an honesty away from their most self-serving sorrow.

GEORGE: Maybe so, maybe so...

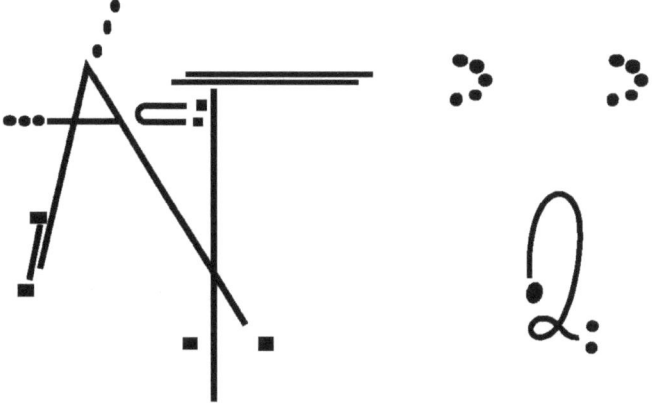

(They are both sitting on an enormous seesaw which instead of simple seats has two incredibly comfortable deep armchairs. He is sitting in a solid red one, and she in a red one with yellow stripes)

GEORGE: Why do I have the impression that the seesaw is the only game a person can play with someone else in which there is no winner or loser in the end?

CONSCIENCE: This doesn't apply to the seesaw of life.

GEORGE: To what?

CONSCIENCE: To the seesaw between a person and his conscience. Here there are no draws looking for a way to convince him that they are worth more than a defeat, only victories and defeats that start cutting logics into shreds, till they discover from which part of theirs man is made.

GEORGE: So they don't care out of which part of their owner they themselves are made?

CONSCIENCE: The self-criticism of a victory or a defeat doesn't think for itself, it only thinks on behalf of its owner. How can anyone defeat his own conscience?

GEORGE: Just by believing that he can defeat her.

CONSCIENCE: And what does that mean?

GEORGE: It means that man has allowed a paradise to exist inside his head, in the middle of which a stunningly beautiful hell lives undisturbed.

CONSCIENCE: It might also mean that when a man believes that his conscience may, even for a moment, become his own adversary, then he has already lost.

GEORGE: I don't know anymore how to make room in my mind so that I too will be able to fit in it along with all those victories and defeats that daily besiege it. I don't know, I really don't know. When my logic makes a mistake I'm just annoyed, while when my soul makes one I suffer immensely.

CONSCIENCE: You humans really enjoy seeing your consciences profusely bleed the truth from their most vulnerable spot!

GEORGE: We are glad to see the doors of our consciences open and close slowly, making sure that they don't let any of the truths that don't want to share their future with us get out. Hence, you consciences produce inside us the huge waves you yourselves have carefully designed through the years, waves that sometimes carry non-stop the truth on their back, trying to have her disembark on our life's shoreline, while other times they can spend endless hours motionless, arm in arm with the silence their mother gave them as a gift.

CONSCIENCE: You know who the mother of truth is?

GEORGE: Authenticity?

CONSCIENCE: Exactly. You should know that consciences daily give birth from scratch to what, because you don't know what else to call it, you dub "my minimal truth". They come and leave it for you at the spot in your life that is both the most physically remote and emotionally central. They leave it there for you so you can touch it, by simply trusting the strength contained in the dawn that's hiding in the first drop of sweat you will believe has a piece of your honesty in it.

GEORGE: The truth we conceal inside us or the one we use to wrap the outer part of our mind so it becomes more likeable, appearing to be more honest, so we can persuade the people around us that we are made solely from something that is only positive?

CONSCIENCE: Both.

GEORGE: Please, don't judge me so easily. You should know that the truth is not equally accessible by everyone.

CONSCIENCE: Don't try looking for excuses in the alibi created by your self-awareness to protect you from the ulterior motives of your intellectual flaccidity.

GEORGE: Tell me, to which of all the truths that flirt with the most beautiful lie that's hidden in the alibi of my self-awareness are you referring to?

CONSCIENCE: The truth I am talking about is not moderate, nor even especially cooperative. It is the one which refuses to live in the middle of the human soul, and only lives in her remotest parts, the ones that contain the great risks and the great pleasures. These are her most jagged cliffs, ready at any moment to fight with anyone in defense of her interests. She loathes the typical, the average, demanding to live only in the absolute which the most extreme parts of her owner's life fell in love with. She stopped long ago being just a truth and is now a cry that has gone to the most inhospitable spot of man's existence and has dedicated her life to try to remake herself from thousands of his favorite whispers. It is these whispers that express the love her owner always had for the mediocre, the ones that demand to represent the courage which since he was young, each time he opened his mouth to speak, tossed his happiness into the trash, hoping it might convince them to stop demanding to gulp him down. Its these whispers she collects one by one each day at dawn and adds them to her own body, making it stronger, more resilient.

GEORGE: How do you convince your life's whispers to remake you from scratch?

CONSCIENCE: By letting them grab from your normality the strongest cries you have and start screaming until they make the walls of your mind shake.

GEORGE: You are right, every average that lives in the dead-center of someone's cowardice is so frayed because it's forced to live constantly struggling to reconcile what the two extremes that gave birth to it, that defined it want. It is constantly exhausted, almost decimated by the endless negotiations with them, trying to convince them to stop arguing about which of the two is superior.

CONSCIENCE: If you want to really hurt a happiness, teach her how to live in the middle of a life. If you want to finish her off, teach her how to think.

GEORGE: Why do you say that?

CONSCIENCE: Because if you retreat a little bit here and a little bit there, you end up living in an castrated happiness, a happiness that can't find the reason she must learn how to feel since she is so good at thinking. Face it. You people force your consciences to live arm in arm with the middle of your life, that spot of hers your mediocrity is constantly trying to convince you not to leave, not even for a second. You see, you are so in love with your survival, that you completely ignore your own honesty, which is patiently waiting a truth away to meet you all over again. You do your best to trim a little bit here and a little bit there, until you shape the final product of who you are into something so smooth and so soft that it can slide and fit in any box your social circle demands that you live in.

GEORGE: What's wrong with survival?

CONSCIENCE: Nothing, you should just be fearful of the kind of happiness that promises you a life which looks like uneventful survival! I am talking about a life where man lives constantly buried deep in the gray hideout provided to him by his life's average, this cunning white line in the middle of every road indicating to every driver what he must do to stay safe.

GEORGE: What are you trying to say, that this line we think is white is ultimately much grayer than we think?

CONSCIENCE: Yes, because when you blend white and black, you end up with a gray which, the moment it's born, will fall at your feet begging you to never explain to it to which of the two colors it owes its existence the most. You see, it does all it can to never discover what it believes in, because it knows that you can't betray something you haven't had time to believe in. Happiness can't survive in the middle of a life, only logic can. True happiness cannot bear to live embracing the average because she never learned how to compromise. The kind of happiness that knows how to negotiate is not happiness at all, it's just mere survival.

GEORGE: Sometimes, unfortunately, I am not quite sure anymore if anything can stand to live in the middle of my happiness except for any emotion of mine that it's not worth feeling. I would really like to believe that nothing can stand it! Please talk to me, though, talk to me about that truth you spoke of, I really need to hear it.

CONSCIENCE: I am afraid that in the middle of your happiness live the only emotions you have which, since you know you can defeat them any time you want, you assume they have no value. Would you like to know why I'm saying this?

GEORGE: Why?

CONSCIENCE: Because the truth I am talking about lives only on a soul's battlements, on her borders with those words reality leaves behind her when she brushes past her owner's tears. It is the truth that is always ready to give all of herself to defend those tears, knowing that she will only get one chance in her life to do it. *(Pause)* Have you ever given birth to a truth, I wonder, that refused from the first moment of her life to believe you?

GEORGE: Now that I think about it, I have regrettably borne many that want to tell the truth only to others.

CONSCIENCE: And what are they telling you?

GEORGE: Words that lose their identity seconds after being born, inches before they reach my ears. *(Pause)* This is the slavery my honesty feels, the slavery in which I rush every morning to clothe the day, before any other emotion of mine that believes in my misery more than it believes in me has time to grab it from my hands. This damn slavery makes me promise each time I leave home to go to work that I won't take her off me for a single minute until I get back late at night. You know, I have been struggling for hours now to persuade my mouth to let me confess something to you. *(He lowers his head)* There are days when I feel so dishonestly intelligent that the price for someone to be next to me is his very truth.

CONSCIENCE: Are these the days you discover that you know how to be both emotionally honest and a liar at the same time?

GEORGE: Even worse. These are the days I discover that I am capable of simultaneously being both mentally honest and emotionally dishonest. They are the days when I start my day casting around me hundreds of those invisible fishing hooks which my logic has baited overnight so I can catch all the innocent souls that believe that I have nothing else hidden in my charm apart from what I don't know how to show them.

CONSCIENCE: You mean those unarmed darknesses that souls hide behind their owner's happiness?

GEORGE: No, I mean the ones they tie on the bumpers they install on their dreams so that they can be sure, in case of an accident, that they will be the ones to be killed first. Face it, dreams that are worth dreaming don't fit in a single night.

CONSCIENCE: Except for those you should have never started dreaming of. Speaking of dreams, did you know that the sharpest curves in a person's life are born straight?

GEORGE: And at some point discovered the freedom of not having to fight tooth and nail to retain their flawless, almost perfect shape. I know, unfortunately I know. For this reason, they surrendered their happiness to the ambiguity of letting randomness define the shape you will have tomorrow.

CONSCIENCE: And who told you that a curve is born with the hope that someday she will be able to be straight?

GEORGE (*In tears*): Why do the straight lines in my life have so much falsehood in them! I want so much to find a way to overcome the gravity of my ambiguity, this perfectly straight line, this suffocating perfection that, from the moment I realized all the possessions it daily provides me, managed to make me believe that I owe her any emotion of mine my own logic is cramming me into an incredibly uncomfortable school desk so I can analyse it until I can no longer understand what I feel. I want to break her in half with a single blow to find out where this massive interior stone wall of my mind begins, which shields my misery from her dreams, especially those she has of me.

CONSCIENCE: You mean to protect yourself from the man she wants you to become.

GEORGE: Maybe, maybe... Will you help me?

CONSCIENCE: To help you, you must first surrender to me the keys to your silence.

GEORGE: You mean the keys to my authenticity?

CONSCIENCE: No, I mean your silence.

GEORGE: How can I give you the keys to a delusion which doesn't express itself, so I don't know what it's made of, I don't even know where it begins and where it ends?

CONSCIENCE: Don't underestimate yourself. You know a lot more about your silence than you think.

GEORGE: But...

CONSCIENCE: You are just afraid to admit it.

GEORGE: Why should I fear my silence?

CONSCIENCE: Because she can blackmail you by keeping inside you everything you have felt and haven't found a way to express.

GEORGE: And what does that mean?

CONSCIENCE: Don't you realize that you have managed to rid yourself of all the words you have uttered, since they are no longer part of you, have long been outside your body, while your cunning silences keep on living all together inside you? Their body weighs you down, makes you emotionally sluggish, denying you the right to walk freely through your life, to touch whatever you wish to touch, to feel whatever you want to feel. You feel as if you are crossing an astonishing meadow abounding with flowers while you are enclosed in a glass box which takes you wherever it wants to go, restricting you to only see but not touch all the beauty that's around you.

GEORGE: What misery!

CONSCIENCE: What's worse is that the meaning each word of yours keeps inside it is poisoning you, since it never stops slowly flowing into your soul, like a ship that keeps on polluting the sea years after it sank.

GEORGE: Is that why every time I blow off steam, every time I let my words take out of my soul the pain that I have inside me, I feel as if I have liberated myself from an enormous weight?

CONSCIENCE: Yes. This way you are being good to yourself, even if you are freeing yourself from a burden that often you don't understand exactly which one it is.

GEORGE: Interesting. But have you seen me throw pieces of myself to my delusions, have you seen with what frenzy they fall upon them to devour them?

CONSCIENCE: Come on, you know that truths only walk around the spots in a man's life where the light has long stopped negotiating with darkness. Don't pretend that you don't understand that every day you become the appetizer of a delusion which, during its course, you yourself will give birth to, to protect yourself from the opinion your favorite catharsis has of you. You will just have to accept that if you want to free yourself from the unbearable pressure you feel that you must constantly hide who you really are in those minutes of each day which refuse to tell you what they want from you.

GEORGE: You know, my lie has figured out that now is the right time to touch me on that spot of my body that no longer enjoys listening to the favorite fairytales my truth tells it.

CONSCIENCE: Come on now. I was always under the impression that you knew that, if you ever managed to convince your stupidity to allow you to live without her for a short time while she dares to walk in your life on her own, without any help from you, her body would not cast a shadow while walking through the long corridors your lies have created at the edges of reality for you to cross.

GEORGE: That's right. That's why I started making the two legs I will use to walk today out of some slightly used truths I found waiting to meet me outside that very important merit of mine which does not believe in me anymore. These steps I will use today to walk to the point of my sorrow where, no matter how hard I try, I will not be able, while embracing my life, to figure out what I feel and, after conquering it, I will rush to squeeze into that place which my very own soul, no matter how hard I pressure her, will refuse to feel. I really need to live a little in an emotional vacuum, in a place that will respect my soul's capacity to only feel when she wants to, a place that won't ask me to feel anything while I'm in it. I really need that! I really need its emotional protection. What liberation, what salvation!

CONSCIENCE: I hope this is the spot in your life which, without realizing it, will ask you to hand over your soul to it at its entrance, like a store where you surrender the bags you are holding upon entering so that you won't be able to steal something and sneak it out while exiting.

GEORGE: That's the one.

CONSCIENCE: You mean to say that to escape from the man your sorrow wants to make you, you must first steal your guilt from your next joy?

GEORGE: I will probably have to become the man who, because he failed to persuade his truth to live with him, ended up becoming the successful burglar of his own lie.

CONSCIENCE: It must be very frustrating to realize that the lie that lives in the most secret part of the sorrow of the people you love discovered before you the fourth dimension of your body, and not only discovered it but will do everything it can to never show it to you. It's so strange to feel that to free yourself from what enslaves you in your life, instead of running as far as you can to get away from it, you must run the opposite way from where you logic commands you and go stand motionless in the absolute center of your soul. There you must wait until she herself starts confiding to you what for some time now she can't bear to hide inside her. Instead of running to escape from what she wants to ask you, you must go to her center and demand the answers she has owed you for years.

GEORGE: Perhaps this way a man's authenticity acquires a place of birth, a homeland, perhaps this way he himself can avoid becoming the lover of his delusions by not falling to his knees and doing his best to convince the lies he's been serving to the people next to him all these years to lend him for the last time the kind of honesty he knows he still has somewhere in him but hasn't found a way yet to convince her to represent him.

CONSCIENCE: Exactly. I feel your very lie, your most capable, your most devious lie having such a great need to give birth to a truth on its least ambitious edge, a truth, though, it will not tell you if you don't apologize to it first for all that you have made it do for you all these years. I always believed that a person's lies live inside him exactly in the same spot where his apologies live. Do you believe that?

GEORGE: Why, I wonder, have we forced the most significant lies in our life to be so demanding, to demand to understand what such a big part, an important part of ourselves refuses to confide to them?

CONSCIENCE: I don't know. Tell me something, though. Why do you believe that your ego has forced your lies to do all they can to convince you that to a certain degree they are invisible?

GEORGE: Since the sunshine in my life is so often invisible, why shouldn't my lies be invisible too?

CONSCIENCE: It turns out that there are times in a person's life when he must not listen to what the twilights all around him whisper to him.

GEORGE: Especially those that have convinced him that they love him. I think that in the end I fear the most those twilights in my life that back off when I go near them, avoiding to talk to me, avoiding to even look me in the eyes, rather than those that don't fear me at all and as soon as they see me coming stand up straight across from me, ready to pounce on me and rip me to pieces.

CONSCIENCE: How did we suddenly start talking about how much you fear your sorrow?

GEORGE: By opening the door to my reality and entering the part of yesterday that demands more from the coming day than I do.

CONSCIENCE: Are you talking about the part of tomorrow that yesterday carries within it?

GEORGE: Of course.

CONSCIENCE: I hope this won't be another discussion you will avoid telling me what material it is made of till its end.

GEORGE: Are you talking about the discussion or the part of yesterday that will be born tomorrow?

CONSCIENCE: I want to know about the former, although I have the impression that you wish to talk about the latter.

GEORGE: Probably. I don't know, maybe that "future yesterday" you are talking about is made of those hopes that don't belong to me anymore, the hopes that believe more in my past than in my future.

CONSCIENCE: There it is again, darkness, look how the damned thing managed to get in between your words.

GEORGE: Why, hane you ever participated in a single discussion about yesterday that didn't include at least one darkness?

CONSCIENCE: Maybe…Perhaps…I don't know if you agree, but I always assumed that your life's darknesses do their best to ensure that you will never know what their exact dimensions are.

GEORGE: Why, do you think they know? The darknesses obtain their dimensions from the stare they get from the greatest fear we have in us the moment we start standing a cowardice across from it and look it in the eyes. These darknesses know how to tear into me and grab it from me, no matter how much I try with all my strength to quickly try to understand what I must do at that moment to resist them, to understand not what I fear, but what I should not fear. I thus came to realize that the darknesses are not produced by the absence of light, but by the absence of courage.

CONSCIENCE: Souls produce the darknesses from any materials they fear the most themselves. *(Pause)* I always believed that darknesses are made by what is left of a self-confidence once you take away the biggest alibi that lives inside her.

GEORGE: Please don't force my fist again to look for the alibi it hid in the intelligence of my cowardice.

CONSCIENCE: Is it time for you to let your fist talk openly about all that it fears in front of any part of your past that demands of you to look more courageous than you really are?

GEORGE: Every fist is an ex smile that no longer knows how to do its job properly.

CONSCIENCE: Maybe it is also a future sorrow looking for a way to get born. Have you ever wondered why you have imprisoned yourself in your own fist?

GEORGE: Faced with your questions, my self-esteem takes a step back and my ego a step forward.

CONSCIENCE: Have you ever asked what your triumphs believe about you?

GEORGE: Please, don't try to poison any part of myself that wants to shape my next smile for me.

CONSCIENCE: No, I won't do that, but please don't forget that true misery is to be unable to explain to the person you became what kind of a person you want to be.

GEORGE: Why is it wrong once in a while to cut up one of your dreams to see what you forgot to put in it?

CONSCIENCE: Ah, you always liked so much the part of yourself that borders midnight!

GEORGE: Why do you want to force tonight to become a false witness for my cowardice?

CONSCIENCE: How do you feel, I wonder, returning back to what you were never able to become?

GEORGE: No matter what you say, today you won't be able to persuade my past to find a new owner.

CONSCIENCE: You would really like to live in the only pocket of your past that has a hole in it, wouldn't you?

GEORGE: Next thought of mine, please unlock me from all that I don't know how to begin to remember. Come my self-awareness, come and please make me a draw that looks like a victory.

CONSCIENCE: I see you're once again ready to become the pimp of your melancholy.

GEORGE: Get out, damn you, from the spot in my head where all my defeats permanently live.

CONSCIENCE: There is no fist that could ever fit between the nightmares of courage and the dreams of cowardice.

GEORGE: Listen. I am not trying to hide anything more in the phrase I will tell you than an argument that uses the most cowardly darkness inside me to convince itself that it is not black.

CONSCIENCE: Stop being a peddler of handicapped realities.

GEORGE: Please, though, let me be the official translator of my lies.

CONSCIENCE: Only if you bought a ticket to where you are going for your truth too.

GEORGE: My beliefs may decide today to take a long trip within me.

CONSCIENCE: Perhaps to try to discover the extent of the desert inside you which all these years, no matter what you do, you haven't been able to cross.

GEORGE: Maybe to also discover the dimensions of my fist.

CONSCIENCE: Perhaps, perhaps…

GEORGE: Speaking of dimensions, do you think that even one of all these sorrows from way back, that once in a while grow like weeds in the middle of my life, has any idea what its actual dimensions are?

CONSCIENCE: They're not simply sorrows. They're feelings of guilt masquerading as sorrows. Besides, I am sure that you know by now that there is no darkness that doesn't know the purpose for which it was born.

GEORGE: Sorrow, sorrow… How much I really need my sorrow! Even though I keep kicking her away, she's always there by my side. The more I drive her away from me, the more I feel the need to immediately apologize to her, to hug her. What is this all about! And don't think that sorrows come to our lives uninvited, we invite most of them ourselves, you might even say that we beg them to come and hang out with us.

CONSCIENCE: Are you saying that man deserves his sorrow?

GEORGE: There are few things that man deserves more than a sorrow that fits into who he becomes every moment of his life to avoid being happy, as if joy is a stain, an intolerable stain that sullies his life. *(Stops talking, as if he had a new idea, then raises his head and looks persistently at the ceiling)* I don't know if my sorrow scares me more than that cursed long silence which gushes out of any moment of my life I let the ambiguity of my sorrow give birth to before I had time to start shaping it the way I wanted to. That damn silence refuses to talk to me every time she comes and sits beside me, unbearably close to me, right next to my soul, demanding, without even addressing me, that I turn around and see in her captivating eyes her determination to not only defeat me, but also to consume me. She has the ability, or rather I have endowed her with the ability to call the clouds fog, the moment eternity, the expiration date beginning. *(Pause)* Why do I like so much to breed inside me those weaknesses of mine which think that they are stronger than me?

CONSCIENCE: Tomorrow is in a hurry for you to show it your shortcomings so it can see which part of yourself it can remake from scratch to make it seem less defective.

GEORGE: You are making me go back to the point in my life I could never get away from.

CONSCIENCE: I am making you kiss on the mouth the part of your personality you have been trying for months now to evacuate as far as you can from your ego's opinion of you.

GEORGE: I feel that my insecurities will in the next few days start putting together their family tree right in front of me.

CONSCIENCE: If you don't want to become a slave to your previous optimism, liberate your logic from the fear that you must use the next version of yourself before you are ready to understand it.

GEORGE: Weren't you the one who always told me that I must stop living on the borders of my private night with my previous optimism?

CONSCIENCE: No, I simply always told you that at some point you must stop adopting the end of your sorrow from its own beginning.

GEORGE: If you want to say something, say it! You want to ask me if I can emotionally afford being what my past wants me to become, don't you? Admit it.

CONSCIENCE: I'm impressed by how many curves can fit in the last straight line in your life that still thinks that it owes its shape to you. Hell, how many delusions can you fit in a truth you're doing all you can so she won't believe in you?

GEORGE: Every time I beat a darkness in arm wrestling, I simply clutch the fear I have in me in my palm and squeeze it until I make it look like my previous cowardice.

CONSCIENCE: Maybe that is how you cowardice disguises herself as a truth that you happen to have the ability to understand what she is avoiding to tell you.

GEORGE: Maybe this is how I manage to translate the winter inside me into my smallest mistake. *(Pause)* How much more ambitious than me can my personal fog become?

CONSCIENCE: An emotional fog's ambition is often to use its body to cover any mistakes with the kind of apologies that know how to buy words that will never be spoken off the account your happiness has opened for your sorrow. These damn apologies do their best to never be able to see the tears they will soon bring forth in the eyes of the people they dominate.

GEORGE: Do you think that this is the apology that every emotional fog owes its owner?

CONSCIENCE: Don't forget that man does not sell serenity to his soul, he just buys it from her.

GEORGE: At what price?

CONSCIENCE: The respect of his silence.

GEORGE: What do you mean?

CONSCIENCE: Have you ever asked your silence what she feels, what she believes about you, every time she hears you speak?

GEORGE: Not disgust, I hope. *(Pause)* My silence has so much loneliness in her, so much damn melancholy!

CONSCIENCE: But isn't that what every person is, the melancholy in every word he never found the courage to utter?

GEORGE: Perhaps also the hope in my next thought which can no longer stand to stay inside me. She wants to run in the narrow corridors my silence has constructed in my mind so she can easily check any thought that passes before her trying to reach, as quickly as it can, the point where mentally my mouth starts. She's in such a hurry to break the iron bars I have installed to ensure that no thought will be able to transform me into a man who, in order to become who he is, was forced to sell the next step in his life to his previous misery.

CONSCIENCE: Perhaps he also sold his previous self along with it.

GEORGE: Perhaps even his true self.

CONSCIENCE: Do you mean the only self that can stand living next to him?

GEORGE: I would really like to be able to live around the clock with the only version of myself that can stand the smell of who I really am.

CONSCIENCE: You could do that if you knew which part of your logic separates each silence from the next words that come out of your mouth. I wonder, do you know which one it is?

GEORGE: The ingratitude my sincerity feels when I ask her to tell me what she thinks of me?

CONSCIENCE: The various alibis hiding in your most cowardly truth. Don't forget that what taught you to climb mountain peaks is fear, not ambition.

GEORGE: What fear?

CONSCIENCE: The fear of betraying the part of yourself you owe to your beliefs.

GEORGE: What…

CONSCIENCE: Why are you looking at me like that? Have you never wondered why, when you sit right next to your loneliness, you seem more alone?

GEORGE: Damn you, I see that today you came ready to flirt with the part of my logic that never learned how to trust the sound of the echo my every word hears while proudly standing and shouting, as loud as it can, before the only wall in my mind which, no matter how hard I have tried, I haven't managed to jump over to see what's on the other side.

CONSCIENCE: Now I understand which means you use to defeat your reality.

GEORGE: Now I think you can understand how I manage to defeat my serenity.

CONSCIENCE: I guess now I can figure out which part of your mind you should return to your authenticity.

GEORGE: I beg you, don't go near my guilt when I am not present.

CONSCIENCE: What phobia of yours are you hiding behind what you are doing your best not to tell me?

GEORGE: None, not a one…

CONSCIENCE: Come on. I can see your unspoken words fighting on the edge of your lips about which one will push another till it falls out.

GEORGE: What happens when reality comes and stands in front of me to announce to me that I am not made of the materials I think? What happens when she stands over me like a strict schoolteacher and starts scolding me because, once again, I cannot understand who I am trying to be?

CONSCIENCE: You just gave your next sorrow the right to move for a short while to the central spot in your life.

GEORGE: Screams of mine, gather all around me! Come, I really need you right now. Where the hell have you hidden them? I need them right away. How do I always manage to confess to you how easily I end up belittling what I can no longer feel? Why can't I stand before the greatest certainty I feel in my life and shout with all the strength in my soul: "I fear you, dam it, I fear you"? Why, why?

CONSCIENCE: Because once you swore to defend from any attack she might suffer from me that delusion which, because you loved her more than any truth, you ended up hating her more than any of your lies.

GEORGE: Tell me, why do I fight so often with my truth?

CONSCIENCE: You don't fight with your truth, you fight with the freedom she offers you.

GEORGE: What freedom?

CONSCIENCE: Man is totally free when he has nothing more to hide behind the image he shows to the people around him, when he has nothing to hide behind the lies he uses to appear to be more real than he is. You see, a person who is truly happy belongs to his truth, while a person who just thinks he's happy is under the delusion that his truth belongs to him.

GEORGE: Don't compel me again today to embrace my worst self in order to discover how many leftovers of my character's beauty I throw every day to my melancholy to persuade her to stop shouting slogans against me.

CONSCIENCE: There's no other kind of happiness except the one you think you don't need.

GEORGE: Yes, I know, I know, you've said so before. The sky becomes invisible for a few minutes before turning blue every morning. Some lines wake up bent out of shape before they slowly straighten out again latter at noon. Please, don't make me sit again in the most uncomfortable spot of my day so you can try to teach me the value of a tear that no longer remembers how to cry. Don't force me to sit across from the whitest full stop I can find while looking through my optimism's dirty laundry to discover all the sounds that can no longer stand being white silences, don't make me sit across from them and stare at them until I'm able to figure out how my loneliness demands to differ from my misery.

CONSCIENCE: I won't, but I will ask you today to persuade your voice to steal any cry from inside you that can't stand to be silent anymore. Don't you understand that you have become the only eraser which your life is using, while constantly going up and down your reality, inspecting all her parts, erasing any part of your freedom it deems no longer suitable for you?

GEORGE: I don't know if I am ready to become the outline of my ambiguity before I become the center of my misery. Isn't this the joy of the eraser a soul almost always holds in her hands, to be able to erase from the next moment of its owner's life the emotions it wants, while leaving others completely intact?

CONSCIENCE: Listening to you struggling to produce in your mind arguments that believe more in the survival of your ego rather than in your happiness, I wonder if in the end there may be a delusion that is more honest than the prefabricated truth you serve reality every morning so she will agree, albeit briefly, to become yours.

GEORGE: I don't know, but the longer I think about it, the more I feel a century of sorrow begin to write its memoirs on what's left of my existence once I remove my most emotionally ambitious dreams. I wonder, can I stand to discover today to what spot in my dreams my soul has moved to avoid seeing me every morning get up and run, as fast as I can, to manage to betray what I am before I turn into what my sorrow expects me to become.

CONSCIENCE: Because she really hopes that this way you might be able to regain the right to transform yourself into a man admired more by his guilt than by his greatest happiness.

GEORGE: Exactly. How can you heal a wound, that doesn't want to discover the reason it hurts?

CONSCIENCE: By embracing the next question that the first tear that's been ready for days now to flow from your eyes avoids asking you, the tear which, seeing the decisions it's made on your behalf pass before you one by one, recognizes the one which believes more in your cowardice than you believe in your own courage. Can you bear, I wonder, to become the bridge your soul will tread on to go stand at that spot of your happiness that insists on surviving a few feet away from you, across from you, a place where truth seems less like slavery, where darkness looks less like what it actually is and starts resembling the freedom that only the faintest candlelight has in it?

GEORGE: I disagree I always felt that every darkness I met in my life gave me a feeling of absolute freedom from the start.

CONSCIENCE: While the light was intolerably suffocating you because it made you realize who you are, where your limits end?

GEORGE: That's right, because the damn thing, by sending its beams, demanded to know everything about me. Light is so indiscreet, so annoying…

CONSCIENCE: Not if you don't have anything to hide.

GEORGE: Come now, everyone has something to hide.

CONSCIENCE: Not those who know out of which part of their heart they have made their happiness.

GEORGE: Sky of mine, how can you stand being so blue, how can you stand not having a single cloud in you? How can you stand not needing to hide even for a moment behind what you are? Will you please let me grab a storm from inside you and, after teaching me how to hold it in my hands, leave it outside my truth's front door to see if she will let me in?

CONSCIENCE: If you want to do something for yourself, I would suggest that you load ten of the most beautiful and, at the same time, overweight lies on your back and start crossing the bridge that leads to what you always thought made your logic seem more handsome than you.

GEORGE: And what will I accomplish this way?

CONSCIENCE: You will be able to understand who you will become if you ever find the courage to combine the catharsis held on your behalf by your most valuable darkness with the side of your mind which the unselfishness of your happiness refuses to visit.

GEORGE: Please, let me go on believing that cowardice is the mirror into which the truth that no longer wants to live the life given to her by her owner demands to look.

CONSCIENCE: You speak as if you believe that you can stand to emotionally strip naked in front of all the different kinds of your cowardice. Can you? Will you cope?

GEORGE: Not before I undress before the one fog in my life which, because I cannot define it, I have allowed to define me.

CONSCIENCE: You are right. Whatever you can't find the courage to define will soon after attempt to define you.

GEORGE: Oh, yes. I've being there already... Anyway, I like feeling that the first thing that the alibi I feed my logic with to stop her from screaming does, as soon as its born on the edge of my mind, is to find the part of the image of myself I show to the people around me when I no longer have anything real to show them.

CONSCIENCE: Hoping that this way it might manage to hide you from who you think you are?

GEORGE: Probably.

CONSCIENCE: I think the first thing it will want to do is to convince you that in it this image of yourself conceals a small treasure which only you deserve to discover.

GEORGE: Every time we talk about this issue, I feel my tears searching inside me to find what they forgot to take with them.

CONSCIENCE: Rightly so, because, ultimately, man does resemble the dreams his delusions dream on his behalf!

GEORGE: I am in no position to scorn something whose value I don't know how to calculate.

CONSCIENCE: The battle's last moment, the grimace of pain from the last hit you suffered while it lasted, will explain to you the true reason you fought. It's incredible, as man grows older, how capable these minutes of his life become at demanding from him to give them another color except the black he has in him, so they can paint his next day anyway they want. These damn moments have the capacity to search throughout his sorrow to find spare parts to repair his optimism without his permission, hoping that this way they will manage to discover those triumphs of his he knows he did not deserve to achieve, the ones he has personally hidden in the warehouses his cowardice built in the most distant place in his mind, so that he does not have to often come into contact with them.

GEORGE: I get so afraid of myself every time I let my mind remember for me! When I let my soul remember for me, I begin to hope again.

CONSCIENCE: I knew you would say that...

GEORGE: Don't be so arrogant. There are times when even fire itself fears its own flames.

CONSCIENCE: I thought you would say its ashes. Poor man, how many locks do you think your life has that you still haven't realized that they can imprison you?

GEORGE: You should see how many locks I have made in my life forgetting to make keys so I can open them afterwards.

CONSCIENCE: Oh, I see...

GEORGE: If you think this will manage to persuade my self-awareness to abandon me even for few seconds to come before you and beg for some of the crumbs of authenticity you offer her from time to time, you are mistaken, gravely mistaken. Talking about locks, at the end of every day of mine only one loneliness fits through the single door which every midnight, just before it locks my happiness in its own darkness, leaves intentionally unlocked. There awaits me the desert I weaved all day from all that happened during its course, during which I didn't have time to realize what I felt before I was forced to express it.

CONSCIENCE: Are you talking about that part of the night that can only fit in it the kind of lonelinesses hidden inside those twilights that don't know anymore how to figure out on their own out which part of the world the sun will come out tomorrow?

GEORGE: That's right. They are determined to wait all night alone until they get a chance to sit before any other human emotion on the edge of the new day, hoping they will manage to learn some news from the very shadows their owners cast passing through the day that just ended.

CONSCIENCE: I like the way you handle what you don't know how to fear.

GEORGE: You see, I am the kind of person who, before trying to conquer the next reality in his life, always makes sure to have already conquered the one version of himself that could not understand which of all my truths it was fighting so hard to grab from inside me. Oh, I remember how difficult it had been for me all those times, and there were many, when I fought tooth and nail to do this without betraying my self's previous version. *(Pause)* As time went by I left many pieces of myself inside them! How the hell did I ended up being so loyal to the part of my character I never managed to believe in?

CONSCIENCE: Aren't you impressed by how fascinated you are by this emotional explosion you feel every time you realize how admired you are by the abyss that lives in you?

GEORGE: That damned emotional explosion you talk about knows how to make me feel that I am doing something which one half of me considers illegal and the other half admirable. It is so good at making me feel that I become the smuggler of my own enjoyment, a man who is willing, in order to please the doubts he has about himself, to end up becoming a false witness of his own sorrow.

CONSCIENCE: It must be really strange to see half of yourself be the main prosecution witness submitting evidence before the other half, in a court presided by you and a jury comprised of all those truths of yours you personally betrayed throughout your life!

GEORGE: Now I am sure. Every man is a wasteland in which he refuses to throw a single piece of garbage.

CONSCIENCE: Except for those he does not know how to pick up.

GEORGE: Maybe those he doesn't know how to throw out?

CONSCIENCE: Maybe.

GEORGE: You damn conscience, you allow only rookie darknesses to participate in the game you like to play so much with every person you intend to dominate.

CONSCIENCE: Honesty is not to hide the truth from others, while happiness is not to try to hide it from your own self.

GEORGE: How many times in a conversation do you want me to enter my mind's oncoming traffic lane and attempt to crash head on with my future to make you happy? How many? Don't you see that I am an image, a strangely happy reflection of my defective triumphs on the face my authenticity shapes every morning out of any weaknesses of mine I didn't use the previous day?

CONSCIENCE: Have you ever considered which part of yourself you would find if you ever managed to break into your melancholy to steal your biggest guilt from inside it? Could you, possibly, believe in one of the dignities you have which believes more in your shortcomings than in you? How can you pretend that you don't see how many different kinds of past have come and sat in front of us while we've been talking, forming a giant wall to stop you from seeing what your next defeat has been trying for hours now to show you? You sit frozen in the middle of your scream trying, without anyone's help, to figure out if the shipwreck you created is worthy of the tempest. You are not there by accident. You came to spawn wounds, you came to set traps, not only for your luck, but also for your most important good qualities. You want so much to prove to yourself that, after completely immobilizing them one by one, you can give your rage the answers you promised it. I always felt so sad seeing people who, once they were freed from their freefall, the first thing they did was to jump.

GEORGE: They may even go hide in the most cowardly part of their life's ascent.
(His Conscience does not respond)

GEORGE: Your words lined up before me one by one to try to wash the wounds of my compassion. I don't know… It could be that the duty of the end of every happy moment in our life is to remind us of the appointment we have with the beginning of the next one.

CONSCIENCE: Could be…

GEORGE: Well, one needs great courage to start looking for the birthplace of his own cowardice. One also needs great courage to start searching for the point in one's sorrow where the part of the worst day of his life which insists on living inside him all year round starts.

CONSCIENCE: So, what are you ready to do about it? Will you do something or will you simply keep on observing your sorrows shape the next minute of your life anyway they want?

GEORGE: I will, I will. I wonder if it's time for me to look in my closet for all my summer clothes, to search all their pockets hoping I'll discover any smile I left in them in the moments during one of those incredible sunsets when, immersed in it I felt like my soul had grabbed with all her strength my body with both hands and shook it back and forth, until she made it feel down to the last square inch of it. These were the magic moments when I didn't care if every smile of mine was forced to disappear as soon as it saw my mind coming from afar holding a yellow eraser, so it could start deleting whatever my soul had written on the body of the moment that had just ended.

CONSCIENCE: For goodness' sake, let your passion come talk to me!

GEORGE: Get over here people, gather round. My self-awareness is giving out autographs today. Shadow of mine, you too come close to me, come, let me tell you one of the most beloved fairytales my future wrote about me.

CONSCIENCE: I don't understand why you insist on standing right in between two sorrows of yours which for days now want so much to duel right in front of you? I sense that your imperfections are relieved every time they see you behead another of your good qualities, just so you can satisfy the ego of your shortcomings and thus persuade them not to start another civil war among them, the one they've been threatening you with for some time now.

GEORGE: I really fear this civil war so much, I really dread it! God damn you, how many winters can you fit in a single word! I wish I could feel, even for a single day in my life, as if all the darknesses will die the moment the first ray of the sun rush over the earth, I wish I could feel that all my own darknesses will die the moment the first ray of the sun starts caressing the dozens of questions the previous night painted on my face!

CONSCIENCE: This is the intelligence of darkness. It always remembers more things than you. That's why you should never toss even the most insignificant piece of your memories into the trash, especially those you cannot figure out what they are trying to make you remember...

GEORGE: Why?

CONSCIENCE: Why? Because they will be useful to you once their own answers decide to throw you into the trash.

GEORGE: How does one approach one's self without scaring him off?

CONSCIENCE: By letting his defeats pick the part of his past in which they want to live from now on.

GEORGE: I sense that a victory is sitting half a self-confidence away from me and has been watching me for a few minutes, unable to decide whether she wants to come closer and talk to me. Why do I have the impression that the end of my triumph demands to instantly soak up every last applause I hold in my palms? What the hell happened suddenly and everything I did right in my life demands to move to the neighborhood inside my head where my biggest mistakes live?

CONSCIENCE: I think today is not the right day for you to answer the questions of those shortcomings of yours you consider the most valuable.

GEORGE: You mean the ones I don't consider shortcomings anymore?

CONSCIENCE: Today is the day you will learn how to get through a winter without asking yourself every minute what its first day wanted to tell you for so long.

GEORGE: What happens when a person's shortcomings believe that they are worth more than him? *(Pause)* I feel the need to grab my adolescence by the hand and start walking with her through my life, until I reach that spot where my shortcomings have erected their own statues. You know, I must tell you that I never learned how to be properly sad, and that's why I don't know how to produce tears that have feelings in them that want to express something other than my sorrow.

CONSCIENCE: Are you one of those people who believe that, before it strikes, an earthquake searches through its body to quickly find out how many other wounds it has, to make sure that when it decides to attack humanity, it will have marshalled all its strength?

GEORGE: Yes, yes… Every time they see me feeling sorry, losing my courage, my shortcomings rush together all over me to lift me in their hands and, while celebrating their victory, celebrate my defeat. By God, I just feel like catching the first earthquake that believes in himself as little as I do, pull him out of the earth, hug him and place my heart next to his so we can both cry until we feel our sorrows start talking to one another, hoping that this way they won't feel the need to attack, to destroy.

CONSCIENCE: There are afternoons when I see you leaving work having gathered from the top of your desk all the tears that didn't get a chance to become truths during the day. You want to take them all home with you, you don't want to leave them behind all alone, and you certainly don't want to throw them away. You take them with you so they'll remind you who you didn't manage to become for yet another day. Upon opening the door of your home, the first thing you see sitting pretty on the couch waiting for you is the biggest lie that can fit in your smallest truth.

    It has brought with it its tool chest, to help you find together by the evening a way to convince your mind to let you sleep, without bringing to you in the middle of the night that ungrateful mirror, for you to realize how much more phonily beautiful than you your image is. Meanwhile, the grand warden of your life, your age, keeps standing speechless a bit further away. It is waiting along with the dozens of pieces of wreckage of yourself you left on the sidewalks of the day that just passed, it is waiting for the last piece to come so they can all ask you together those questions you didn't find the courage on your own to ask yourself.

GEORGE: How I wish the outer side of truth resembled the inner side of the freshest delusion I just bore today. For yet another day it unfortunately refuses to help me.

CONSCIENCE: Right. I really like seeing you not believe that there such a thing as a virgin delusion. I really like watching you carefully examine the gaze she lends you to look at your greedy past, which won't, not even for a second, leave the side of the loot that your defeats keep on bringing you nonstop.

GEORGE: Memory has such high emotional maintenance costs!

CONSCIENCE: She is anxiously searching in the dusty warehouses of your mind for a fairytale, any fairytale, to give it to you so you can tell it to your truth and so be able to put her to sleep, because you know that if she doesn't fall asleep you won't be able to either.

GEORGE: Now I understand how it is possible for me to feel like I am simultaneously becoming the blackest cloud in the sky and the fiercest wave in the sea.
CONSCIENCE: Now is the time for you to realize once again that a blank page will never find its own end.

GEORGE: Why?

CONSCIENCE: Because from the time it is born it refuses to define its beginning. It is the time of day you realize that an unwritten misery never wants to know where she put the reason she was born, because she knows that when a man decides to destroy his past, he automatically ends up destroying the part of his future that he will need the most.

GEORGE: Yes, those are the moments when, crying without shedding tears, I avoid betraying what my honesty was after me all day to tell me, namely which pieces of my soul I have to offer her today to make her happy.

CONSCIENCE: If only you could find out every morning what your soul wants from you…

GEORGE: What does a person do at the end of the day with all those emotions he left unused, emotions he managed to feel but out of shame, out of cowardice, he never took them out of his body, never shared them with anyone?

CONSCIENCE: All together they make a makeshift winter who, just before midnight, will rush to his side to hug him, to make sure that he won't manage to escape his freezing embrace for a single moment all night.

GEORGE: As I grow older, I become convinced that ultimately people owe to themselves every evening, before they go to sleep, to not throw away the biggest delusion they developed themselves during the day before they sit with it and listen to what the poor thing wants to confess to them. Could it be that man is doomed to never be able to be as true as his truths?

CONSCIENCE: I would say that one can never be as true as the truths he rushed all through his life to produce every time he was attacked by his most accomplished lies.

GEORGE: I know, I know, you don't traverse a darkness by starting to walk right into it, but by starting to hope. For some reason, though, I can not sufficiently explain, the eraser of my life today decided to stop erasing and begged me to teach it how to write.

CONSCIENCE: I hope that the starting line of this happiness of yours is not already in debt to her end.

GEORGE: I hope it doesn't owe anything to the finish line of my latest misery. Please don't tell me that this is the way the apology of a happiness that never found the courage to dare begins!

CONSCIENCE: Perhaps, perhaps… Now that I think about it some more, perhaps this is the way the apology of a full stop that's doing its best to not put an end yet begins.

GEORGE: Is it possible that my sorrow is ready today to start digging up the dreams she buried in the battles they had not realized they were fighting on my behalf all these years?

CONSCIENCE: Is it perhaps time for you to unload the story of your life on the hard questions your future has for you?

GEORGE: Please tell me, reassure me that what I feel this moment is the misery of a perfect beauty and not the happiness of a perfect ugliness.

CONSCIENCE: If you want to find the answer to that, toss into the trash the part of your radiance which only you can understand the reason it never wanted to belong to you.

GEORGE: By finding this answer, though, might I, perhaps, discover that I can live for the rest of my life in between the war that my two biggest lies have declared on each other?

CONSCIENCE: Yes, you might, as long as you keep your promise to them to not try to take the side of any of the two.

GEORGE: Do you think any man can be the boss of his lies?

CONSCIENCE: Why, do you think that anyone can be the boss of his sorrow?

GEORGE: I don't know, probably not. Wasn't it you who always told me that man betrays no one more often than he betrays himself?

CONSCIENCE: I said "his past", but never mind. If you noticed, the spare parts of your logic in which you never believed, want you to give them another chance to assemble you from scratch.

GEORGE: How?

CONSCIENCE: By letting an entire century of sorrow, which, having managed to defeat your ambiguity, is now sitting frightened behind the strongest conviction you have in your life and has been sneaking looks at us from the beginning of our conversation, wait for you to call it to your side and welcome it to the next embrace you will find in your compassion.

GEORGE: In the memories of people who don't know how to remember correctly, the shipwrecks of history have started reliving those triumphs they never got a chance to achieve. I wish I could understand what the massive wall I've been building since my youth in the middle of my mind, to keep my sorrow away from my next mistake, has been whispering to me for years now.

CONSCIENCE: Maybe today is the day.

GEORGE: Yes, yes, maybe today is the day for the full stop I will use at the end of that sentence of mine whose time has come for me to utter to decide on its own to be born all white.

CONSCIENCE: An all-white full stop! I like that. I might even like it as much as those vertical sheer drops that insist on being born horizontal.

GEORGE: You might, you might at that…

THE END

Cover painting
If you want to really hurt a happiness, teach her how to live in the middle of a life. If you want to finish her off, teach her how to think.

Back cover painting
There are days when I feel so dishonestly intelligent that the price for someone to be next to me is his very truth.